REAL WRITING

Functional Writing Skills
for Intermediate Students

**David Mendelsohn
Joan Beyers
Maureen McNerney
Marian Tyacke
Michael Carrier**

Dominie Press, Inc.

Publisher: Raymond Yuen
Editor: Pamela Breyer
Cover Design: Patti Bergin-Gallup
Illustrations: Carol Webb Atherly, Pantec Art, T. Andrews

© Dominie Press, Inc. 1992

Reprinted 1994

Reprinted 1997

All rights reserved. No part of this publication may be reproduced or transmitted in any form or by any means, electronic or mechanical, including photocopy, recording, or any retrieval system, without the written permission from the publisher.

 Dominie Press, Inc.
1949 Kellogg Avenue
Carlsbad, California 92008 USA

ISBN 1-56270-008-1

Printed in U.S.A.

4 5 6 7 8 9 10 W 98 97

Table of Contents

Acknowledgements iv
Introduction To Students vii
Introduction To Teachers ix
Unit 1:   Informal Letters 1
Unit 2:   Giving Information 6
Unit 3:   Describing People 14
Unit 4:   Describing Places & Objects 21
Unit 5:   Describing the Past 25
Unit 6:   Comparing & Contrasting 29
Unit 7:   Invitations & Directions 33
Unit 8:   Preferences & Choices 38
Unit 9:   Instructions 42
Unit 10: Future Plans 48
Unit 11: Formal Letters 52
Unit 12: Reporting 58
Unit 13: Summarizing 64
Unit 14: Advising & Warning 70
Unit 15: Persuading 76
Unit 16: Describing Processes 82
Unit 17: Telling a Story/Narrating 91
Unit 18: Expressing Opinions 97
Unit 19: Agreeing & Disagreeing 102
Unit 20: Building an Argument 107
Answer Key 110

Acknowledgements

We would like to thank our colleagues John Archibald, Marjatta Holt, Kate Kellar and Gord Nore and their students for field-testing this material. Their feedback has been invaluable.

Finally, we would like to thank Jenny for checking sources.

David Mendelsohn
Joan Beyers
Maureen McNerney
Marian Tyacke

The publisher would like to thank the following for permission to reproduce or adapt copyright material:

Liberty Lines Express, Inc.
The Canadian Press
Newsday, Melville, New York
Punch Publications Ltd: cartoon by Ken Pyne
Mr. Jules Feiffer: cartoon
The National Magazine Company Ltd.: Davitt Sigerson review
United Press International

Syndication International Ltd.
The Essex County Standard
The Evening Gazette
Bricent Language Courses Ltd.
Brooke Bond Oxo Ltd.
Dateline International Ltd.
Sovereign Holidays
Times Newspapers Limited
Adrians Estate Agents
Ashe Laboratories
Camera Press Ltd.
Mr. T. Parks
The Controllers, Her Majesty's Stationery Office
Embassy of the United States of America
Courier Printing and Publishing Services Ltd.

Photographs Courtesy of:
Portland Community College, Portland, Oregon
Eastman Kodak Company, Rochester, New York
La-Z-Boy Chair Company, Monroe, Michigan
Quaker Oats Company, Chicago, Illinois

Introduction To Students

Here are some notes to help you understand this book and what you can learn from it.

The book is designed to help you improve your written English. It gives you practice in reading and understanding, reorganizing the language you already know, and writing about a variety of topics in many different ways.

The book is designed for intermediate students who wish to be able to write the different kinds of things people need in an English-speaking country. The work at the beginning is easier than at the end.

This book gives you real writing tasks to help you function in English.

How the Book Is Organized

There are 20 units, and each one contains different types of exercises. They are all organized like this:

Section A: **Texts,** diagrams, and pictures give you the information you need to write about a particular subject. The text also gives you examples of the language you will need.

Section B: **Glossary** explanations help you understand words that you may not know from the text.

Section C: **Comprehension** questions check whether you have understood the text.

Section D: **Analysis** questions are more difficult than Comprehension questions. You are asked to think about the text in more detail, and to work out answers from hints and clues in the text.

Section E: **Discussion** questions give you practice in thinking and talking about the wider meaning of the text and suggest other related topics that you could think about. You are also given the opportunity to use the new vocabulary you have learned.

Section F: **Language Practice** teaches you how to change sentences around, and to construct more complicated sentences. You will learn different types of sentences for different types of writing.

Section G: **Writing Practice** exercises give you practice in written English and train you to use the type of writing you are learning in that unit. These exercises prepare you for the real writing tasks.

Section H: **Writing Task** exercises ask you to use all the information and language you have learned in the unit. After you have done the Writing Practice exercises, you will be able to do one or more of the Writing Tasks. Tasks include writing letters, reports, summarizing, describing, and comparing things – all real writing!

How To Use the Book

You should work through all the units in the order they appear in the book.

If you are working through the book with a teacher, then he or she will tell you which parts of each unit to spend more time on and which to leave out. You should also work on your own by using the glossary and, if necessary, a dictionary to study the texts in advance. Also, some of the exercises have the answers printed at the back of the book, so you can do them on your own and then check the answers yourself. But ask your teacher first. An asterisk (*) marks the exercises that have answers at the back.

If you are working on your own without a teacher, then you must decide which exercises to do. If you have a lot of time, you should do them all. Otherwise, spend more time on Sections A, B, C, F, G, and H. When you have finished the exercises marked with *, you can check the answers yourself. For longer pieces of writing, you should try to find someone who writes good English to read through and correct them. You will probably not have time to do *all* the writing tasks in section H.

Good luck with your writing!

Introduction To Teachers

This course has been designed for ESL students at the intermediate level. The units are graded, with the earlier units being easier than the later units. The course aims at providing students with training and practice in functional writing tasks. More specifically, the course aims to:

- develop students' competence in the use of specific functions of language such as expressing an opinion, giving instructions, etc.
- develop students' understanding of the differences between written and spoken English.
- make the students aware of sociolinguistic variation such as levels of formality, short forms, etc. and when to use them.
- help students develop and practice specific writing skills such as composing a letter, summarizing, writing a report, etc.

At the same time, the book develops and practices these general language skills:

- reading for factual information and inferencing
- vocabulary extension in the topic areas dealt with in the units
- oral summary of text material
- oral presentation of information and argument for discussion
- oral interpretation of visual material

Organization of the Book

There are 20 units, each consisting of the following categories of exercise and practice material. There are slight variations in some units, but the format is essentially:

A. **Text** and/or visual stimulus: to provide students with the information they need for the Writing Practice, along with examples of the written forms they will need to use.

B. **Glossary:** simple explanations of lexical items from the text giving the meaning specific to the context.

C. **Comprehension** (questions)

D. **Analysis** (questions)

E. **Discussion** (questions)

F. **Language Practice** (exercises)

G. **Writing Practice** (exercises)

H. **Writing Task(s)**

How To Use the Book

Each unit contains a wide range of practice material, and it may not be possible to cover all the work in class if class time is limited. The teacher should then decide which exercises are most appropriate to the specific needs of his or her students and which can be omitted. Similarly, many of the exercises can be given to students to do as homework or self-study work. The writing tasks at the end of each unit are meant to be alternatives from which the student or the teacher chooses the most interesting or most appropriate. Students in intensive courses may have the time to do more than one of the tasks.

The units vary slightly in length and level of difficulty, becoming progressively longer and more difficult. Because of this, and the obvious variation in classroom situations, it is not possible to specify how much class time would be needed to complete a unit.

This textbook does not claim to cover all aspects of writing. Consequently, the classroom teacher who knows his or her students' levels will probably find that there are things taught in some units that are redundant for their students, or that there are omissions. For instance, a particular function might call for the use of a lot of passive forms (Describing Processes – Unit 16), and the class may have demonstrated a lack of command of the passive. When this occurs, the teacher is urged to supplement the book with additional activities. Grammar is not explicitly taught in this book.

The following notes explain the function of each type of activity:

A. Text

(and/or visual material)

This gives students a model for written work along with facts or opinions they can use. Where possible, this should be prepared by students in advance and reread in class in connection with Sections B and C. However, teachers should not spend too much time on the reading because this would take away from the time for writing.

B. Glossary

The explanations given here should be adequate for most students. In the classroom situation, students should be encouraged to help each other with unfamiliar items, and the teacher should try to elicit explanations from the class before explaining anything. It should be noted that the glossary explains the meaning of a word as it appears in this specific context.

C. Comprehension

These questions are designed to be used as oral checks on students' understanding of the main points of the text. They can be supplemented by the teacher's own questions suited to the level of the class. If time is limited, these questions can be assigned along with the text as preparatory homework. When used in class, students should ask the questions of each other, and also perhaps formulate their own questions. If these questions are too simple for a particular class, they should be left out.

D. Analysis

These questions are designed to develop students' skill at extracting information and/or inferencing from the text or visual material at a more detailed level than normally dealt with by comprehension questions. They can be answered orally in class, or in writing. Where necessary, students are encouraged to speculate or hypothesize as to meanings "behind" the text.

E. Discussion

These questions give the students an opportunity to discuss the wider implications of ideas or information in the text, thus preparing them for the written exercises. The questions should be dealt with orally, and the teacher should decide how far the discussion element of the unit should be developed. The main purpose of the discussion is to enable students to increase their awareness and knowledge of the topic.

F. Language Practice

The exercises under this heading give practice in the various structural and functional aspects of language that students will need to use in their real writing tasks. Examples of the same forms also occur in the various text models that are given, and the teacher should draw the students' attention to the way these forms are used. The exercises are designed primarily for oral work, but could be given in writing. Some exercises (marked with the symbol *) are keyed at the back of the book, making it possible for students to work on these independently. Please bear in mind, however, that when more than one answer is possible, the answer key provides only one suggested answer.

G. Writing Practice

In this section there are activities such as linking sentences, sequencing, reporting, summarizing, etc. that give the students models and practice exercises needed to do the written tasks at the end of the unit. This section prepares students for the specific forms and techniques used in writing and draws attention to the differences between spoken and written English forms. The texts and other stimuli used as models in this section supplement the main text of each unit, giving examples of the same language constructions used in a wider variety of situations.

H. Writing Task(s)

The tasks are designed to help students practice the writing techniques they have learned and developed by working through the unit. The tasks are meant to be alternatives, and the teacher should decide which would be most suitable for the students.

Note that the explanations and instructions in the units are directed at the students, suggesting how they should approach the material. This is not meant to replace the teacher's guidance although some students may wish to study on their own. This technique gives students practice in understanding instructions, and allows the teacher to assign certain tasks for homework or private study without having to explain the nature of the exercise.

The writing tasks are aimed at improving the students' ability in functional writing. At a later stage, students would need to be trained in the organization and format required for different genres.

Final note: some of the texts could be interpreted as "sexist." We would like to point out that such texts are used only to make a point for discussion and in no way reflect the views of the authors.

Union County College
Libraries
Due Dates

User ID: 29354005361512
Library name: ELIZABETH

Date due: 5/14/2015,23:59
Title: Real writing :
functional writing skills for
inte
Item ID: 39354001350830

Thank you
*

1. INFORMAL LETTERS

A. Text

> Nov. 18
>
> Dear Carolyn,
>
> Thanks for your letter. It was great hearing from you. Seems like ages since I last saw you.
>
> Glad you're having a good time at college. Your new courses sound very interesting, but too much like hard work for me!
>
> I've also been working hard moving into my new apartment. I've repainted most of it and put up new pictures and posters, etc. Now I'm saving up for furniture to match the paint!
>
> Hope you'll drop in when you come home after exams.
>
> Your friend,
> Bill
>
> P.S. The new address is:
> 624 Wilson Ave. #1812
> White Plains, NY 10110

B. Glossary

ages	=	a long time
saving up	=	keeping (not spending) money
to match	=	to look good with the color of the paint
poster	=	cheap copy of a picture
drop in	=	visit (informally)
give me a call	=	telephone me

C. Comprehension

1. Where is Carolyn?
2. What has Bill just done?
3. What is he going to do soon?
4. What does Bill want Carolyn to do?

D. Analysis

1. How do you think Bill knows that Carolyn is taking new courses?
2. Are Bill and Carolyn friends, relatives, or lovers? Is it possible to say?
3. Where does Carolyn's family live? Is it possible to say?

E. Discussion

1. Why do people write letters to each other?
2. What is the difference between a letter and a telephone call?
3. Do you prefer to write to people or to call them? Why?
4. This letter is handwritten. A lot of letters are typed. Do you think one kind is more interesting or more friendly? Why?

F. Language Practice

1. Shortened Forms

When we talk or write to friends, or talk quickly, some words become shorter and some words are left out. Look at this example from Bill's letter:
Bill wrote: *Seems like ages since I last saw you.*
The long form: *It seems like ages since I last saw you.*
Now shorten these sentences in the same way:*

  a. I am glad you're having a good time.
  b. I hope you can come to the party.
  c. Would you like some iced tea?
  d. Do you have any suggestions?
  e. Do you want a copy?

2. Another type of shortened form is the contraction. Parts of words are left out and replaced by an apostrophe.

I have becomes **I've**
They are becomes **They're**

Shorten the **has/have/am/are/is/not** words in the same way:*

a. I am saving to buy a car.
b. She has bought a VCR.
c. They could not help me.
d. He is very young.
e. We have found the answer.
f. They are hungry.

G. Writing Practice

1. Being Informal (see also Unit 2)

When we are speaking or writing to people we know well, we use informal language. Sometimes we shorten words, use different words, or leave words out. Look at the first sentence of this informal letter:

Thanks for your letter. Seems like ages since I saw you.

In a formal letter this would be:

Thank you for your letter. It seems like it has been a long time since we met.

So *thanks* and *ages* are more informal or friendly. *Seems* is more informal than *It seems*.

Using the list of formal and informal words provided and using contractions, rewrite the formal letter below to make it friendly. Note: Sign your name only; you do not need to print it. (Juan Perez is writing to Simon Velasques.)

Formal	Informal
proposition	plans
thank you	thanks
discuss	talk about

Dear Mr. Velasques:

Thank you for your letter. I was very pleased to hear from you, as it has been a long time since we met. I hope you are well. I would like to discuss your business proposition. Please call me or visit if you are in the area.

Yours sincerely,

Juan Perez

2. Letter Forms

Look again at the letter in Section A. Look at the shape of the letter:

	date
opening greeting	

letter

	closing signature

Practice the letter form given above. Write the date, the greeting and the closing signature for a letter to your parents or to a close friend. It is not necessary to write the actual letter.

3. Parts of a Letter

Informal letters have different parts, with different phrases for different things. Below are some examples.

a. Thanking the letter-writer:
   Thanks a lot/very much for your letter.
   It was nice to hear from you.
   I was really happy to hear from you.

b. Asking about health or news:
   How are you?
   I hope you're okay.
   How's your job?

c. Giving news:
   I've been away a lot lately.
   I finally got my driver's license.

d. Making suggestions/invitations:
   Can you come for the weekend?
   We'd really like you to spend a few days with us.

e. Closing:
   Love (if you are close to the person you are writing to) or just sign your name.

H. Writing Tasks

1. Write a letter to an old friend you haven't seen for more than a year. Use the letter form and letter parts that you have learned, and invite your friend to visit you.
2. Below is a letter from some friends of your parents. Write back to them. Don't forget to answer all their questions.

April 19th

Dear Jose,

We got a letter from your mom and dad last week, but we haven't heard from you in a long time. How are you doing? What are you up to now? Are your exams over? Are you looking for a job? Getting one is very tough these days.

When are you going to come and see us? We've got a new car and could take you sightseeing. You'd have a great vacation! Just let us know when and we'll be at the airport to meet you.

By the way, Tim says Hi.

Love,

Cmila & Rod

---

3. Your aunt in Philadelphia sent you a very nice present. Write a letter to her thanking her for it, and arrange a time when you can go see her.

2. GIVING INFORMATION

A. Text

SPEND THE SUMMER IN THE UNITED STATES!
AMERICAN LANGUAGE VACATIONS, INC.

We specialize in English language vacations for young people, because they have special needs and interests — and our vacation courses are organized for just those interests:

- A special teaching program that doesn't repeat the lessons you had at home but builds on what you have learned and extends your English.
- A special social program that makes sure you meet a lot of people so that you can practice your English – with lots of sports activities, theater trips, etc.
- Special teachers and social organizers are on duty all day, every day, to make your vacation enjoyable and useful.
- Specially chosen families welcome you to their homes, so you find out how American people really live.

Students coming to our schools in the U.S. will receive for their course fee:

Language classes — three hours of instruction per day, Monday through Friday, in groups of a maximum of 15. Grouped according to level of English.

Accommodation with carefully chosen families. Includes all meals.

Our social directors are always ready to help with advice on leisure activities, and our office staff will help with any accommodation problems.

INTERESTED? Fill in the application form now, or write for further details to:

American Language Vacations, Inc.
452 West 4th Street
New York, NY 10802
U.S.A.

B. Glossary

accommodation = somewhere to stay
fee = price
receive = get

C. Comprehension

1. How many hours of English will you get in a week if you take this course?
2. Where will you live if you take this course?
3. How many meals per day are included in the price?
4. What kind of people work for American Language Vacations aside from the teachers?

D. Analysis

1. Why does the advertisement stress that the maximum number of students in a class is 15?
2. What does this course offer that other courses do not?
3. The advertisement mentions "accommodation problems." What do you think they mean by this?

E. Discussion

1. Why do you think people go to the U.S. for summer courses? Is it to learn English, or to take a vacation?
2. If you took this course, what would you expect to do, to see, and to learn? What people would you meet?
3. Would you rather stay in a hotel or with a family? What difference would this make in your vacation?

F. Language Practice

1. Expressing Your Preferences

Below is an example of the way you can explain that you prefer doing one thing:

read/watch TV

I **like to read** but
I**'d rather watch** TV.

  (I'd = I would)

Make sentences from these words in the same way:*

  a. listen to records/go to a concert
  b. watch TV/go out
  c. go to baseball games/play baseball
  d. cook dinner/go out
  e. take a bath/take a shower

2. Unfinished Actions

If you started to do something in the past, and you're still doing it, then you can use the **have been doing** form. Look at this example:

I **started studying** English three years ago.
I **have been studying** English for three years.

Now change these sentences in the same way:*

  a. I started learning Spanish two years ago.
  b. Juan started living in San Francisco twenty years ago.
  c. We started attending this school ten days ago.
  d. I started working in Toronto a week ago.
  e. Kim started playing the guitar a year ago.

G. Writing Practice

1. Giving Information

Here is the application form for a summer course with American Language Vacations, Inc. Fill in the information. If you don't have any health or diet problems, leave the spaces blank.

Application Form

Please print

Last Name _____ First Name _____

Date of Birth _____
                Day   Month   Year

Sex: Male _____ Female _____

Address _____
         Number   Street   Apt. No.

_____
City   State   Country   Zip Code

Telephone _____
           (Area Code)   Number

Native language _____ Native country _____

Dates you wish to attend: <u>June-July</u> ☐ <u>July-August</u> ☐

Please list any dietary requirements: _____

Please list any health problems: _____

Signature _____

In case of illness or accident, A.L.V. Inc. should contact:

Name _____ Address _____

_____ Telephone _____

Please make checks or money orders payable in U.S. currency to
AMERICAN LANGUAGE VACATIONS, INC.
Paid by (if other than student) _____

Check ☐   Money Order ☐

2. Expressing Preferences

You have sent your application form to American Language Vacations, Inc., but they want some more information from you. They want to know what you would like to do. This is the letter they have written to you:

---

452 W. 4th St.
New York, NY 10802

April 23, 1988

Dear Ms. Thu:

Thank you for your application form. A place has been reserved for you in the summer course. In order to finalize social arrangements, we will need some additional information. Would you please let us know which sports activities, if any, you would like to participate in? Also would you let us know what your preferences are in terms of movies, theater, or historical places. Finally, if you play a musical instrument or sing, would you be interested in being part of a concert evening which we are hoping to organize?

If there are other activities which you like but which have not been mentioned above, or if you have other interests or hobbies which you would like to see as part of the social program, please let us know.

We are looking forward to meeting you.

Sincerely,

J. Elias
President
American Language Vacations, Inc.

You want to write back to give them the information they have asked for. Here is part of the letter you should write – fill in the blanks yourself.

(Write your address here)
(Date)

Dear Mr. Elias:

Thank you for your letter of April 23rd. I am glad you are saving a place for me in the _____. I am looking forward to it. I am interested in sports, and my favorite is _____. I also enjoy going to _____. Although I like _____, I would rather _____ when there are no English classes. I am also very interested in the concert evening. I could _____. My other hobbies are _____ _____, and I hope that when I am in the U.S. I will be able to _____.

I look forward to _____.

Sincerely,

_____
(Write your name here)

3. Being Formal (see also Unit 1)

When you are writing to someone you do not know, you should use more formal English than when you are writing to a friend. For example, to a friend you would write:

See you soon!

But in a formal letter you would write:

I look forward to seeing you.

Here are some more examples:

Friendly	Formal
Thanks for your letter.	Thank you for your letter.
I'd like to . . .	I would like to . . .
Can I . . .	Would it be possible to . . .
Let's go to . . .	We could go to . . .

Now use the formal phrases above to rewrite this letter. Imagine you are writing to someone you don't know well, so the letter must be more formal. The person's name is Lillian Sanchez.

---

24 River Road
Miami, Florida 33301

Dear Lillian,

Thanks for your letter. Guess what? Next weekend I'm going to be on Long Island. Can I stay with you for a few days? Let's go to a play on Saturday night — my treat! If the weather is nice, I'd love to spend a day at Jones Beach. Give me a call and let me know if this is okay.

See you soon, I hope.
Your friend,
Joan

H. Writing Tasks

1. The school has found a room with a family for you. Write a formal letter to the family explaining who you are, what your interests are, and what you will be doing on your vacation. Write the letter to Mr. and Mrs. Kovac, 95 State Street, Brooklyn, NY, 11205.

2. Pretend you have finished the course. Now you want to tell the course organizers what you thought of the course. Write a formal letter telling them what was good and bad, what you did, and what you liked best. Use the address from the text at the beginning of the unit.

3. A friend of yours is starting his own summer school and wants you to write the advertisement for him. Look at Section A again, and write your own advertisement. Choose a new name for the company.

4. You are applying to colleges in the U.S. in order to continue your studies. Write a formal letter to the Admissions Office of the college below, giving some information about yourself, what you want to study, and how good your English is. Request an application form. Here is the address:
    State University
    North Campus
    Los Angeles, CA 90007
    U.S.A.

3. DESCRIBING PEOPLE

A. Text

Robert Zimmerman was born in North Hibbing, a small mining town in Minnesota, in 1941. In high school he dreamed of becoming a rock'n roll star and taught himself how to play the guitar. However, he changed his mind when he heard the music of Woody Guthrie, a well-known folksinger. He then started writing his own songs and took them to the CBS record company in New York City, telling them his name was Bob Dylan. His first record was produced in 1962 and made him famous almost overnight.

What was it that made this thin young man into a world-famous star at the age of 21? It certainly wasn't his voice, which even his fans found rough and hard. The answer was in the songs he sang. Unlike most pop songs of the time, Dylan's songs had something to say about the world and about people. Songs like *Blowin' in the Wind* and *The Times They Are A-Changin'* criticized the ideas of older people, especially the wars in which they had been involved. With his long, straggly hair and his scruffy clothes, Dylan stood for the rebellion of young people against the rules and ideas of their parents.

Dylan made many successful records up until 1966, when the famous *Blonde on Blonde* was produced. Soon after that he had a serious motorcycle accident and "disappeared" for two years, living a quiet life with his wife and children. When he finally produced a new LP in 1968, his fans were surprised by the change in style — the music was much softer and the songs were not so harsh.

Many fans of Dylan were not very happy with this LP *(John Wesley Harding)* or with the records that followed over the next few years: *Nashville Skyline, Self-portrait, New Morning* and *Planet Waves.* There were some good songs on all of these, but many people felt he had lost the power to write songs that you could think about. It was only with the production of *Blood on the Tracks* in 1975 that Dylan seemed to return to the level of *Blonde on Blonde*, made almost ten years before. In the same year he produced the LP *Desire*, which was his first really successful record in a long time. He also started to give concerts again, playing with a large electric band.

That same year Dylan's wife left him, and this might have made him work harder. In fact, some people believe that it was his unhappiness at this time that helped him to write better songs. This unhappiness can also be seen in Dylan's first film, *Renaldo and Clara*, which was produced in 1978, and which describes both his life as a singer and his marriage. The film is 4½ hours long!

Fans of Dylan have become used to his changes of style, from folksinger to rock group leader to film producer. There is no doubt that he will continue to change and surprise his audiences.

B. Glossary

fans	=	supporters; people who like an artist
pop	=	popular; liked by many people
criticize	=	to find fault with
straggly	=	long and dirty
scruffy	=	messy
rebellion	=	a fight against established ideas
LP	=	record
band	=	group of musicians

C. Comprehension

1. How old was Dylan when he first became famous?
2. What was his real name?
3. When did he become interested in folksinging?
4. Why did he "disappear" for two years?

D. Analysis

1. What made Dylan different from singers before him?
2. What made his songs so popular? What does the text suggest?
3. Read the text again and write down the words and phrases used to describe Dylan. Put them into two groups:
   a. what he is like (appearance, personality)
   b. what he has done
4. What ideas of older people do you think Dylan and his fans criticized?

E. Discussion

1. Dylan's records are bought by people who do not understand much English. Why do you think this is true?
2. Dylan, like many other singers, has sold millions of records all over the world. Why do you think pop or rock music has become so popular?

F. Language Practice

It is not interesting to describe people with only one word, such as:

He is clever.

To make our meaning clearer and our sentences more interesting, we use qualifying words which make the first word stronger or weaker:

He is **very** clever. (stronger)

He is **pretty** clever. (weaker)

Here is a scale of qualifying words from strong to weak:

She's **extremely** intelligent.

She's **very** intelligent.

She's **pretty** intelligent. (informal)

She's **intelligent.**

She's **not stupid.** (informal)

Now complete these sentences. Choose one of the qualifying words or decide not to use one, depending on the sense of the sentence. Remember, if you want to use the last example, you must change the word given to its opposite. For example, **clever** becomes **not stupid.***

   a. That was a(n) **interesting** film — the best I've seen this year.
   b. The Ford Tempo car is a good buy for the money, but it's **expensive.**
   c. Despite criticism from the newspapers, the president's speech was **popular** with businessmen.
   d. The actors' performance was **good** for the first night of the production.
   e. He's **intelligent,** but not enough to become a professor.
   f. I was surprised when I met the director. He's **young** — only 20 years old.

G. Writing Practice

1. Describing Words

There are different kinds of words for different kinds of descriptions. Find out what this list of words means, and try to fit the words into the groups in this table. You must decide if each word is positive or negative, and if it describes physical details, personality details, or is a description of work done.

successful	famous	generous
sensitive	scruffy	inefficient
tall	unoriginal	aggressive
ugly	arrogant	

	POSITIVE	NEGATIVE
PHYSICAL DESCRIPTION		
PERSONALITY DESCRIPTION		
DESCRIPTION OF WORK DONE		

2. Describing Faces

Look at these people. A few of their features have been described. Write a short description of each face, including physical details and suggestions about the personality behind the face.

3. Biography

A biography is a description of what a person has done in his or her life. Here is an example of an actor's short biography:

Malcolm-Jamal Warner first started acting when he was nine years old. One of his first roles was in *Alice, Is That You?* with the Inglewood Playhouse in Los Angeles. As a fifteen-year-old, he auditioned for the part of the son, Theo, on the *Bill Cosby Show*. The show is very popular and Malcolm-Jamal Warner is now very well known.

Now write similar short biographies for these two actors:

Arnold Schwarzenegger
- born in Austria, 1948
- came to U.S. in 1968
- Mr. Universe at age 20
- attended University of Wisconsin
- now very successful in real estate
- has acted in many films and is a U.S. citizen

Marilyn Monroe
- born 1926
- real name was Norma Jean Baker
- grew up in California in the San Fernando Valley
- became a famous movie star and acted in many films
- married baseball great Joe DiMaggio
- took her own life in 1962

H. Writing Tasks

1. You are meeting some friends of your parents at the airport, but they don't know what you look like. Write a short letter describing yourself and your appearance.

2. Your best friend is trying to get a very good job and would like you to write a reference for her. Write a description of her personality and explain why she should get the job of Sales Manager.

3. Here are some facts about Muhammad Ali. Use these, and any other information you can find about him, to write a short biography of the famous boxer. Add your own opinions to the facts, as in the text at the beginning of the unit.

- born in Louisville, 1942
- won his first fight, 1959
- given contract in 1960
- became Muslim in 1964
- was divorced in 1966
- in 1967 he refused to join Army and lost his boxing license
- got license back in 1970
- in 1974 won title of World Champion back from George Foreman
- lost title to Leon Spinks in 1978
- retired from sports a millionaire

4. DESCRIBING PLACES & OBJECTS

A. Text

FOR SALE

A beautiful 4-bedroom house, built in 1979, on Williams Avenue. This house stands on a wooded lot (55′ x 110′) away from the road. There is a large flower garden and a beautiful lawn. The house is only about 1 mile from downtown, and the train station is also very close.

The house has gas heat. Upstairs, there are four bedrooms and two bathrooms. Downstairs, there is a dining room and a very large living room. The kitchen is next to the dining room and comes with appliances. A hallway leads from the kitchen to the front door, with a guest bathroom to the left. The basement has a large family room, a laundry room, and a storeroom. There is also a two-car garage. The house has recently been decorated and painted.

Cost: $175,000

Further information from: Heathertree Realtors

B. Glossary

wooded lot = a piece of land with many trees
lawn = grass
appliances = machines that do a certain job in the home, such as a washing machine

C. Comprehension

1. What is in the garden?
2. How far is the house from downtown?
3. Where is the guest bathroom?
4. What is used to heat the house?

D. Analysis

1. The house is not quite new, so someone has lived there and is now moving out. What reasons could there be for them to move out?
2. The information in the text is for people who might want to buy the house. Why is information about the train station important?

E. Discussion

1. In North America, most of the houses are owned by the people who live in them. In other countries, many people rent their houses. What are the advantages of each system?
2. Some people prefer to live a long way from the city in a house with a garden. Others like to live in apartments in the middle of the city. What are the good and bad points of each?

F. Language Practice

Describing

When we are describing, we can say either:

The house has four bedrooms.   The house has a family room.
             OR   OR
There are four bedrooms in the house.   There is a family room in the house.

Now change these sentences to read like the second sentence in the examples above:*

a. The house has two bathrooms upstairs.
b. The hallway has a guest bathroom to the left.
c. The kitchen has appliances already in it.

G. Writing Practice

1. Expanding Descriptions

The text is a long description of a house. The agent wrote it after making notes. He or she expanded the notes into a description:

Notes
big garden/lawn/flowers

Description
There is a large flower garden and a beautiful lawn.

In the same way, use these notes to write a description of a condominium you want to sell.

2 bedrooms/living room/dining room/12th floor balcony/facing south/ near downtown/10 min. walk from bus station/dishwasher/wall-to-wall carpet/gym and pool in basement

2. Writing Practice

Here is a plan of another house that is for sale. Use the plan and the information given and write a description like the one at the beginning of this unit: Wilson Avenue/built 1977/ lot size 75' x 190'/ $295,000

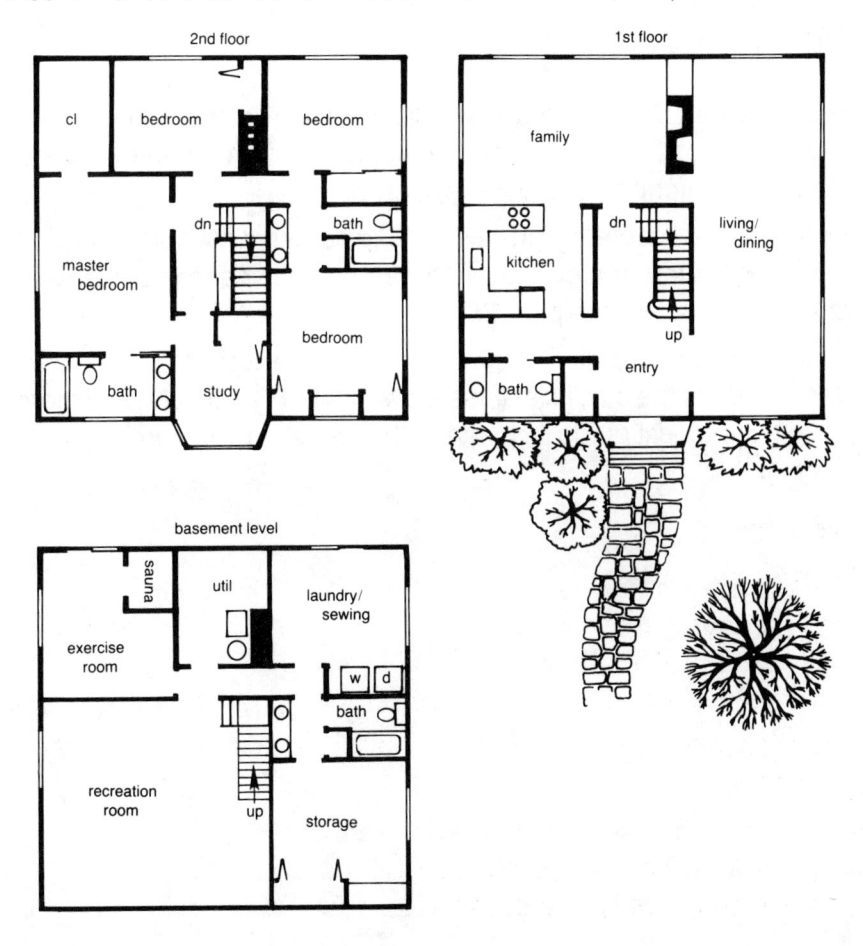

3. Exaggerating

Sometimes people exaggerate in descriptions. They say something is better than it really is. Read the examples below.

Normal	Exaggerated
a nice house	a wonderful house
a pretty garden	a beautiful garden
good value for the money	outstanding value for the money
a comfortable chair	a really comfortable chair
a fast car	a very powerful car

Rewrite this description of a stereo and exaggerate it. Use the words above and any other exaggerated words you know.

> This is a good record player with a nice design. It is a good value for the money, and has some special features. As well as speakers, there are headphones which are comfortable to wear. This system produces good sound, with a lot of power. We suggest you listen to it when you have time.

H. Writing Tasks

1. You work for a big company that sells color televisions. You must write a good description of the new model that just came in. You can exaggerate a little. Here is the information you have been given:

   PY911/new portable/weighs 23 lbs./big screen (21")/computerized controls/can be adapted to stereo system/can use car battery/3-year warranty/80-channel capacity/cheap ($425)

2. The city where you live wants to bring more tourists to the area. Write a description of the city, its sights, and what you can do and see there. This will go into the tourist guide, so write to the tourists using *you*.

5. DESCRIBING THE PAST

A. Text

The Olympic Games

Everyone has seen or heard about the Olympic Games at some time, either in Mexico, Moscow, or Los Angeles. Most people know that the Greeks started the Games. But many people are unaware of the whole story.

The first Olympics took place nearly 3000 years ago, in the year 776 B.C. Many different sports were played, including boxing, running, and throwing the discus, but there were fewer sports than in the modern Olympics. People came from all over Greece to watch the Games at Mount Olympus, and even cities or states that were fighting wars stopped them for the duration of the Games.

The Games were held every five years until they were stopped by the Romans in A.D. 393. They had continued for such a long time because people believed in the idea behind the Olympics: that a healthy body produced a healthy mind, and that the spirit of competition in sports and games was better than the competition that caused wars.

After the Romans stopped the Olympics, that idea was lost for nearly 1500 years. Then in 1894 Baron Pierre de Coubertin had an idea. He thought it would be possible to start the Games again, inviting athletes from different countries to create a spirit of peace and healthy competition. Many others felt this was worthwhile, and on April 6, 1896, the first modern Olympics were held in Greece. Only 50,000 people saw these Games, but the rest of the world soon became interested, and since 1900 the Games have been held every four years in a different country. Only three Olympics were cancelled because of war — in 1916, 1940, and 1944. The biggest Games were in Tokyo in 1964. More than 5700 athletes from 94 countries competed.

B. Glossary

unaware of	=	not knowing
discus	=	a round, flat object thrown by athletes as far as possible
duration	=	the period of time from beginning to end
spirit	=	feeling, idea
competition	=	taking part in a game or sport, and wanting to win
create	=	to make
worthwhile	=	worth doing; the effort would not be wasted

C. Comprehension

1. Who started the first Olympic Games?
2. What was the idea behind the Games?
3. How were the new Olympics different?
4. Why did some Olympics not take place?
5. Why do you think the Games are called the Olympic Games?

D. Analysis

1. Look at the different dates in the text. Use them to make a list of the most important things that happened in the history of the Olympics. The list has been started for you.

    776 B.C. – The first Olympics

2. In the original Olympic Games, people stopped fighting wars to take part. What difference do you notice in the modern Olympic Games?

E. Discussion

1. Why do you think sports are so popular? What makes them so interesting?
2. Many people do not take part in sports but love to watch them. Why do you think these people prefer watching to playing?

F. Language Practice

1. Describing the Past

One way of describing the past is with sentences like:

The Greeks started the Olympic Games in 776 B.C.

But if we want to stress the action and not the person who did it, we use the form:

The Olympic Games were started by the Greeks in 776 B.C.

The Greeks started the Olympic Games in 776 B.C.

The Olympic Games were started by the Greeks in 776 B.C.

OR

The Olympic Games were started in 776 B.C.

Note that it's not always necessary to use the *by* phrase.

Now change these descriptions of the Games in the same way:*

   a. The Romans stopped the Games in A.D. 393.
   b. The athletes played many different games.
   c. Fifty thousand people saw the Games in 1896.
   d. The organizers cancelled the Games in 1916.

2. Describing Changes

When something has changed, or was a habit in the past, we can describe the past situation in this way:

He **used to live** in London.
I **used to bite** my nails.

Describe these changes in the same way:*

   a. People watched the Games at Mount Olympus.
   b. The Greeks stopped their wars to go to the Games.
   c. They held the Olympics every five years.

G. Writing Practice

1. Sequencing

When describing the past, it is important to get everything in the right order. This description of the life of writer Ernest Hemingway is in the wrong order. Rewrite it in the correct sequence, and put the dates on the left.

- wounded in Austria 1918
- shot himself in Idaho, USA 1961
- won Nobel Prize for *The Old Man and the Sea*
- first book published 1925
- born 1898
- lived in Cuba just before WWII
- published *The Old Man and the Sea* 1952
- worked as journalist in WWII

2. Expanding

Below are some facts about another author. Join the facts together into longer sentences using these words:

   when   **before**   **after**

Write your sentences like the examples below.

When John didn't get a raise, he quit his job.
Before going to college, Kim worked at a gas station.
After bowling a perfect game, Victor became the club champion.

Here are the facts to use:
- **a.** His father died.
  He left school to go to work.
- **b.** He started working as a steamboat pilot in 1857.
  He went west to help his brother in 1862.
- **c.** He wrote *Tom Sawyer*.
  He became a famous author.

H. Writing Tasks

1. You have applied for a job as hotel manager, and you have to write a description of your life. Include age, education, what jobs you have had, etc. The description doesn't have to be true.

2. Write a description of a disaster you have seen or heard about. Describe what happened, when it was, what you saw, and how it ended. Examples: a car accident, plane crash, earthquake, or fire.

3. Find out as much as you can about a well-known person (actor, politician, pop star, etc.) that you find interesting, and write a description of their life and what they have done. You can use the Hemingway description as a guide.

6. COMPARING & CONTRASTING

A. Text

Which car is best for you?

Name	Coral	Bella
Basic Information		
Country of origin	United States	Japan
Price	$7575.00	$7990.00
Gas consumption a) miles per gallon b) liters per 100 km	 28 10.01	 32 8.71
Maximum speed	105 mph	102 mph
Number of doors	4	2
Seating capacity	5	5
Standard/Optional Equipment		
Reclining seats	standard	$220.00
Tinted glass	$128.00	standard
Rear window defroster	$175.00	standard
Stereo AM/FM radio	$200.00	$95.00
Power brakes	standard	standard
Power steering	standard	$370.00
AM radio	standard	not available
Extra Costs		
Tax	8%	8%
License plates	$35.00	$35.00
Delivery	$195.00	$300.00
Comments of the test driver	Comfortable but a little noisy	Quiet and safe but not very comfortable

B. Glossary

country of origin	=	country in which the car is made
gas consumption	=	the amount of gas used
reclining seats	=	seats that can move to let you lie down
power (steering/brakes)	=	helped by the power of the engine
standard	=	included in the basic price
optional	=	extra luxuries you can buy for the car

C. Comprehension

1. Which car comes with tinted glass windows?
2. Which car has the most standard equipment?
3. What did the test driver think was bad about each car?

D. Analysis

1. If you take the total cost of each car, including price, extra costs, the cost of all optional features and tax, which is the cheaper car?
2. What are the advantages of buying a car in which much of the equipment is optional?
3. How do you explain the difference in delivery charges?

E. Discussion

1. The text comparing the two cars gives a lot of information. Which do you think are the most important pieces of information when buying a car?
2. Which one of these cars would you choose if you had the money to buy one? Give your reasons.

F. Language Practice

1. Comparing

Here are some of the sentences we use when comparing two things. For example, we can compare the two cars in the text:

The Coral is **smaller than** the Bella.
The Bella is **not as big as** the Coral.
Although the Coral is **cheaper,** its gas consumption is **higher.**

Now write three sentences like these, also about the two cars.*

2. Connecting

Here is one way to connect short sentences in comparisons:

The Rolls Royce is the most expensive car made in Britain. It is the most reliable car.

The Rolls Royce **is not only** the most expensive car made in Britain, it is the most reliable **as well.**

Now write two sentences comparing the two cars in the text, using the same sentence form.*

G. Writing Practice

1. Recommending (Using Comparison and Contrast)

When we recommend something, we usually explain:
- why it's good
- why it's better than the others

Here are some examples:

Flora's Flower Shop — fresh and dried flowers/fast free local delivery
Sweet Scents Flower Shop — excellent variety of fresh flowers/world-wide delivery

- I'd recommend Flora's Flower Shop because it has both fresh and dried flowers.
- The Sweet Scents Flower Shop is better than Flora's because it offers world-wide delivery.

Now write two short recommendations — one like the first example and one like the second example for each of the following:

a. Alfi's Restaurant – good food/world famous chef
   Pierre's Restaurant – reasonable prices/beautiful decor
b. Barbara's Beauty Shop – up-to-date styles/free coffee
   Better Image Beauty Shop – friendly staff/comfortable atmosphere
c. The new Rolling Stones album – more songs than before/more instruments used
   The new Bruce Springsteen album – excellent sound quality/an interesting cover

2. Complaining

If you buy something that is not as good as it should be, you can complain. You compare what you expected with what you actually got:

This digital watch is supposed to give the date, but it doesn't.

Using the same form, complain about the problems you have had with this watch:

What it's supposed to do:
- light up at night
- have an alarm
- be waterproof
- need one new battery a year

What it does:
- light is not working
- doesn't beep
- stops under water
- needs four batteries a year

H. Writing Tasks

1. Make a table (like the one comparing cars) of the good and bad points about going camping instead of going to a resort for your vacation. Compare the different situations and make a choice at the end.

2. You have bought a color television, but it doesn't work as well as you expected. Write a letter to the manufacturer complaining about it.

3. Here are two small motorcycles. The Maxi is French and the Flexi is Italian. You are comparing them for a magazine. Read the information about them and then write a description showing the good and bad points of each. You can make up extra information to add to the description.

Maxi
- very heavy
- fast on hills
- uncomfortable
- good brakes
- double headlights
- reliable
- expensive

Flexi
- light
- cheaper than average
- hard to start
- bad on hills
- cheap replacement parts
- comfortable to ride
- easy to steal

7. INVITATIONS & DIRECTIONS

A. Text

> *Mr. and Mrs. J.P. O'Malley*
> *request the pleasure of your company*
> *at the marriage of*
> *their daughter Megan*
> *to*
> *Roger Davis*
> *on July 27th*
> *at St. Martin's Church*
> *at 11:00 o'clock*
> *Followed by a reception at*
> *The Regency Hotel*
> *Laurel, Pennsylvania*

For those guests coming from out of town, here are directions for finding the church and the hotel:

Driving from Baltimore, take 83 North. Follow the signs to City Center until you come to a hospital on your left. Immediately after the hospital make a right onto a one-way street. Take the first left, then turn left again by Woolworth's. About 200 yards further, on the right, is a parking lot. Park in the lot, since there is no parking outside the church. When you leave the parking lot, continue down the same street and turn right at the corner. You will see the church on the corner on your left.

To reach the Regency Hotel, turn right from the parking lot (same as for the church) then left at the corner. Drive about half a mile and turn left where the road ends. When you come to a school, turn right, and look for a gas station on the left. Take the first road on the right across from the gas station. The hotel is at the end of the road.

B. Glossary

request the pleasure of your company = want you to come (formal)
directions = instructions for finding a place

C. Comprehension

1. Who is getting married to Megan O'Malley?
2. Look at this map. It shows the town where Megan and Roger are getting married. Read the text again and draw a circle on the map for the positions of the church and the hotel.

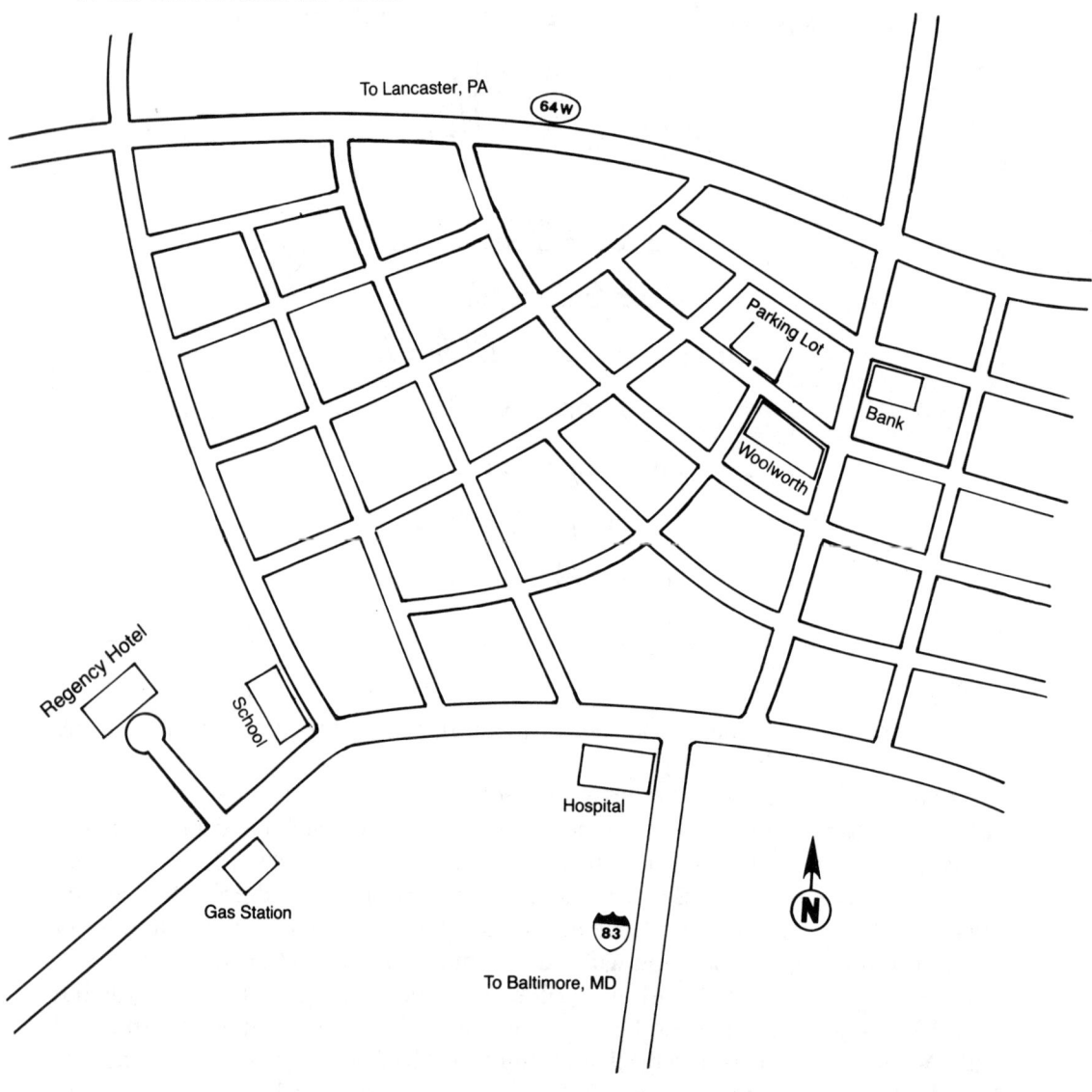

D. Analysis

1. Why do you think directions are given for people driving from Baltimore?
2. Roger does not live in this small town. Why do you think the wedding is here?
3. Where do you think the Davis family lives?
4. What can you guess about the size of the town from the invitation?

E. Discussion

Discuss how people are invited to weddings and what weddings and wedding receptions are like in different countries.

F. Language Practice

1. Invitations

Look at the invitation in the text:

Mr. and Mrs. J.P. O'Malley request the pleasure of your company at the marriage of their daughter Megan

This is very formal and would not be used except for special occasions such as weddings. Normally when speaking or writing to people we know, we use sentences like:

Would you like to come to dinner?

How would you like to come to dinner tomorrow?

How about dinner at my place tomorrow?

Note: These are all informal, but the last one is less formal than the other two.

Now write invitations for the following situations:*

   a. You are planning a picnic by a lake.
   b. You are going camping for the weekend.
   c. You are going to the theater on Friday.

2. Refusing an Invitation

Accepting an invitation is very easy. You thank the person and say yes. Refusing is more difficult because you need to give a reason. Here are some examples:

That's very kind of you, but I've already planned something else. (formal)

I'd love to come, but I have to work.

Sorry, but I'm meeting some friends. (informal)

Now use sentences like these to refuse the invitations you made in Section 1.*

G. Writing Practice

1. Timetables

You are staying in an apartment on Third Avenue and 33rd Street in Manhattan. Your friend is visiting you. He has an appointment at 1:15 p.m. on Saturday at Third Avenue and 91st Street. You have to go out early, but he has asked you to leave him directions about how to get to his appointment and what time he should leave. Using the bus map and schedule below, write him a note telling him what time to catch his bus. (The bus stop is right outside your apartment.)

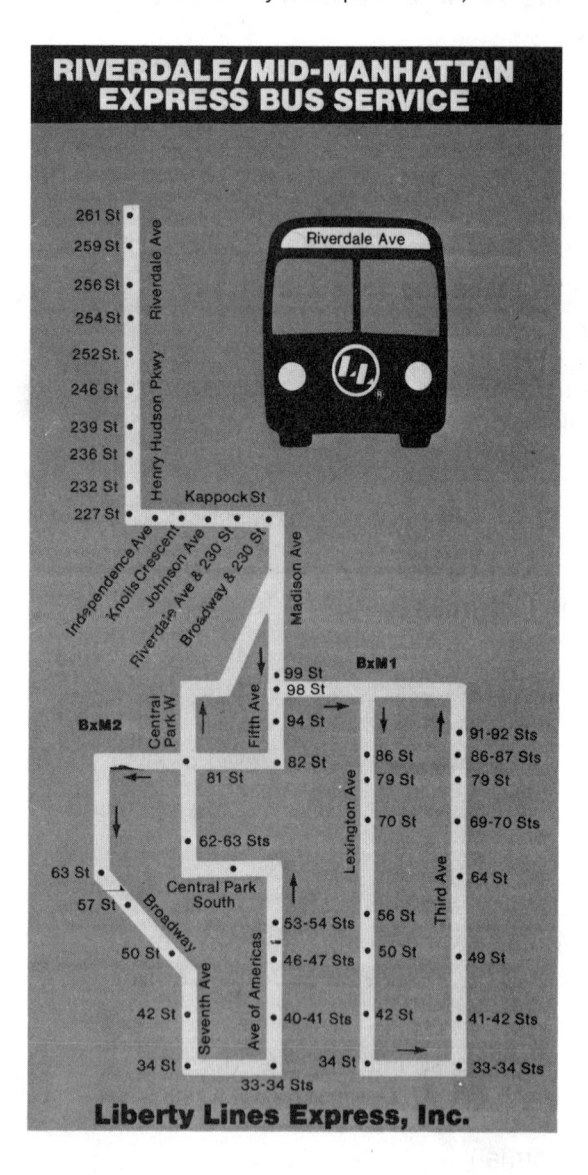

RIVERDALE/MID-MANHATTAN EXPRESS BUS SERVICE

EAST SIDE MANHATTAN TO RIVERDALE AVENUE & INWOOD

	Travel Time in Minutes
Third Avenue between 33rd & 34th Streets	0
Third Avenue between 41st & 42nd Streets	2
Third Avenue S.E. corner of 49th Street	4
Third Avenue S.E. corner of 64th Street	7
Third Avenue between 69th & 70th Streets	9
Third Avenue N.E. corner of 79th Street	11
Third Avenue between 86th & 87th Streets	13
Third Avenue between 91st & 92nd Streets	14

Monday Through Friday

7:40	**1:10**	**4:00**	**5:05**	**8:07**	**8:00**
8:15	**1:30**	**4:10**	**5:10**	**6:15**	**8:20**
8:45	**1:50**	**4:20**	**5:15**	**6:22**	**8:40**
9:15	**2:10**	**4:28**	**5:20**	**6:30**	**9:00**
9:45	**2:30**	**4:34**	**5:25**	**6:40**	**9:20**
10:15	**2:45**	**4:40**	**5:30**	**6:50**	**9:40**
10:45	**3:00**	**4:45**	**5:35**	**7:00**	**10:00**
11:15	**3:15**	**4:50**	**5:40**	**7:10**	**10:30**
11:45	**3:30**	**4:55**	**5:45**	**7:20**	**11:00**
12:15	**3:40**	**5:00**	**5:52**	**7:30**	**11:30**
12:45	**3:50**		**6:00**	**7:45**	**12:00**

Saturday

7:45	10:45	**1:45**	**4:25**	**6:30**	**9:15**
8:15	11:15	**2:15**	**4:45**	**6:50**	**10:15**
8:45	11:45	**2:45**	**5:05**	**7:15**	**11:15**
9:15	12:15	**3:15**	**5:25**	**7:45**	**12:15**
9:45	12:45	**3:45**	**5:45**	**8:15**	
10:15	**1:15**	**4:05**	**6:05**	**8:45**	

All buses serve Inwood on Saturday and Sunday.

Sunday

9:15	12:45	**3:15**	**5:45**	**8:15**
10:15	**1:15**	**3:45**	**6:15**	**9:15**
11:15	**1:45**	**4:15**	**6:45**	**10:15**
11:45	**2:15**	**4:45**	**7:15**	**11:15**
12:15	**2:45**	**5:15**		

AM — light   **PM— bold**

COMMENTS, SUGGESTIONS, INQUIRIES: We invite inquiries, as well as suggestions, constructive criticism, and commendations. Please write to: Customer Service, Liberty Lines Express, Inc., Post Office Box 624, Yonkers, New York 10702; or phone (212) 652-8400 Extension 308 weekdays between 9 A.M. and 5 P.M.

Liberty Lines Express, Inc.

2. Giving Directions

The text at the beginning of the unit gave directions only for people driving from Baltimore. Look at the map again and write directions for people coming from Lancaster.

Here are some more expressions we use when giving directions:

Turn left at . . .
Take the first left . . .
When you come to the _____, turn right.
At the light . . .
At the corner . . .
Go straight until . . .

H. Writing Tasks

1. You are planning a party to celebrate moving into a new apartment. Write a letter to a friend whom you have not seen for a year, and invite him/her to come to the party and stay for the weekend.

2. Some friends from out of town are coming to visit you, but they don't know your town. Write them a letter giving directions to find your house.

3. You have received a letter inviting you to the wedding of someone you don't know very well. You can't go, so you write a polite letter refusing the invitation. Make up your own reason for not going.

8. PREFERENCES & CHOICES

A. Text

Jodi Nichol is 18. She would like to work in the movie business as a makeup artist when she graduates from high school. But first she has to save enough money. Here Jodi talks about money and how it affects her life:

"I used to get $15 a week allowance from my parents, but because that wasn't enough and I got bored on Saturdays, I decided to take a part-time job. Now I work in a donut shop from twelve-thirty until five-thirty. I make $20 for that, $10 a week pocket money, and $2.50 an hour every time I babysit. I spend most of it on clothes and makeup, subways and buses, and going out to clubs.

"My parents don't really have a lot of money, but you wouldn't say they were poor, either. We get lots of clothes and things — well, not lots, but enough. I guess we're OK, but it would be nice to have enough money to hire cleaning help. I'd like a decent life-style when I leave home: a nice apartment, good furniture and up-to-date clothes. I suppose $400 a week would be enough for me to live comfortably. I wouldn't want to be really rich because then you're more likely to get robbed or mugged."

B. Glossary

allowance	=	spending money given by parents
makeup	=	general word for lipstick, mascara, etc.
mugged	=	attacked, beaten and robbed
up-to-date	=	modern

C. Comprehension

1. Does Jodi work full time? What else does she do?
2. Why did she decide to get a weekend job?
3. What does she have to do before she can get a job as a makeup artist?
4. Why wouldn't Jodi want to be very rich?
5. If her parents had a little more money, what would Jodi like them to spend it on?

D. Analysis

1. How much money would you need each week to live comfortably?
2. Do you think Jodi will become a makeup artist?

E. Discussion

1. Do you agree with Jodi that rich people are more likely to be mugged?
2. Jodi earns $20 for five hours of work in the donut shop. This would be $160 for a 40-hour week. Do you think it is a fair salary or not? How does it compare with the amount she would like to make each week?

F. Language Practice

1. Giving Preferences

A simple way to show which of two things you prefer is to use:

I**'d rather be** smart **than** rich.
I**'d rather go** swimming **than** play tennis.
I **prefer** the country. (in general)
I**'d prefer to go** out.

Note: 'd = would
Prefer can be followed by both nouns and verbs:

prefer + noun
prefer + to + verb

Now answer these questions using one of the forms above:*

a. Which car would you rather have – a Corvette or a Ferrari?
b. Which do you prefer – white or whole wheat bread?
c. Would you rather be a politician or an artist?
d. Would you prefer more money and less free time in your life, or more time and less money?

2. Contrasting

To contrast two ideas, you can use:

This car is cheap. That car is expensive.
This car is cheap**, but** that car is expensive.

Note: Use a comma (,) before *but* when combining two sentences.

Now make sentences contrasting these things or situations:*

a. Westerns – interesting / love stories – boring
b. Beethoven's music – good quality / pop music – garbage
c. Traveling by car – fast, expensive / walking – cheap, slow

G. Writing Practice

Preferences

1. Look at the text again, and write a description of Jodi's preferences – what she prefers to do in her free time; what she would prefer to do in the future.

2. Here are some notes on two different color televisions.

   Write a description which contrasts the two, and say what you prefer about each one:

   Synchronic
   - real wooden cabinet
   - 14" screen
   - 2 speakers
   - $379

   Techmatic
   - imitation wood
   - 21" screen
   - 1 speaker
   - $524

3. Choosing a Job

   There are many things to think about when choosing a job. For example:
   - salary
   - hours
   - length of vacation
   - physical or mental work
   - outside, or in an office
   - travel
   - free car with the job
   - work on the weekend

   Using these ideas and the contrasting sentences, describe and contrast these two jobs. Explain which you would prefer and why.

   a. Doctor
   b. Airline pilot

H. Writing Tasks

1. You have to write an advertisement for a bicycle that will explain why it is better than others. Contrast it with Model X and Model Y and explain why everybody would prefer to have your bicycle. It is called the Cyclone.

2. You are looking for a job, and you have gone to a job agency. They have asked you to describe what kind of job you would like to do and what kind you would not. Contrast them in a short report.

3. You want to take a summer language course. The school you wrote to for information has two campuses. One is downtown in a large multi-cultural city where you will have to find your own place to stay. The other is outside of town in a beautiful area where student housing is available. Write a letter saying which you would prefer to go to and why.

4. Look at the two advertisements below for summer vacation accommodations. Write a description comparing and contrasting them.

SUNSATIONAL TOURS

Coral Reef Hotel

This recently built luxury hotel is only five minutes away from the casino and the International Marketplace. A free shuttle bus transports you to a private beach nearby, or to a championship golf course. Elegant dining in the Startop Restaurant has live music nightly. Tennis courts, a pool and a poolside bar add to your vacation enjoyment. Your air-conditioned room has two double beds, and a private bathroom with a tub and shower. Price per person (shared room): $879 for 7 nights. No special rates for children.

Pirate's Cove Resort

This cabin resort is located in beautiful Pirate's Cove. Two-bedroom cabins with kitchen and bathroom (with showers) open onto the white, sandy beach. Our snack bar is open throughout the day, and you can buy food and beverages at our grocery store. There is also a swimming area for small children.
Price per cabin (4 people): $1250 for 7 nights.
Extra occupancy: $250 per adult
$150 per child

9. INSTRUCTIONS

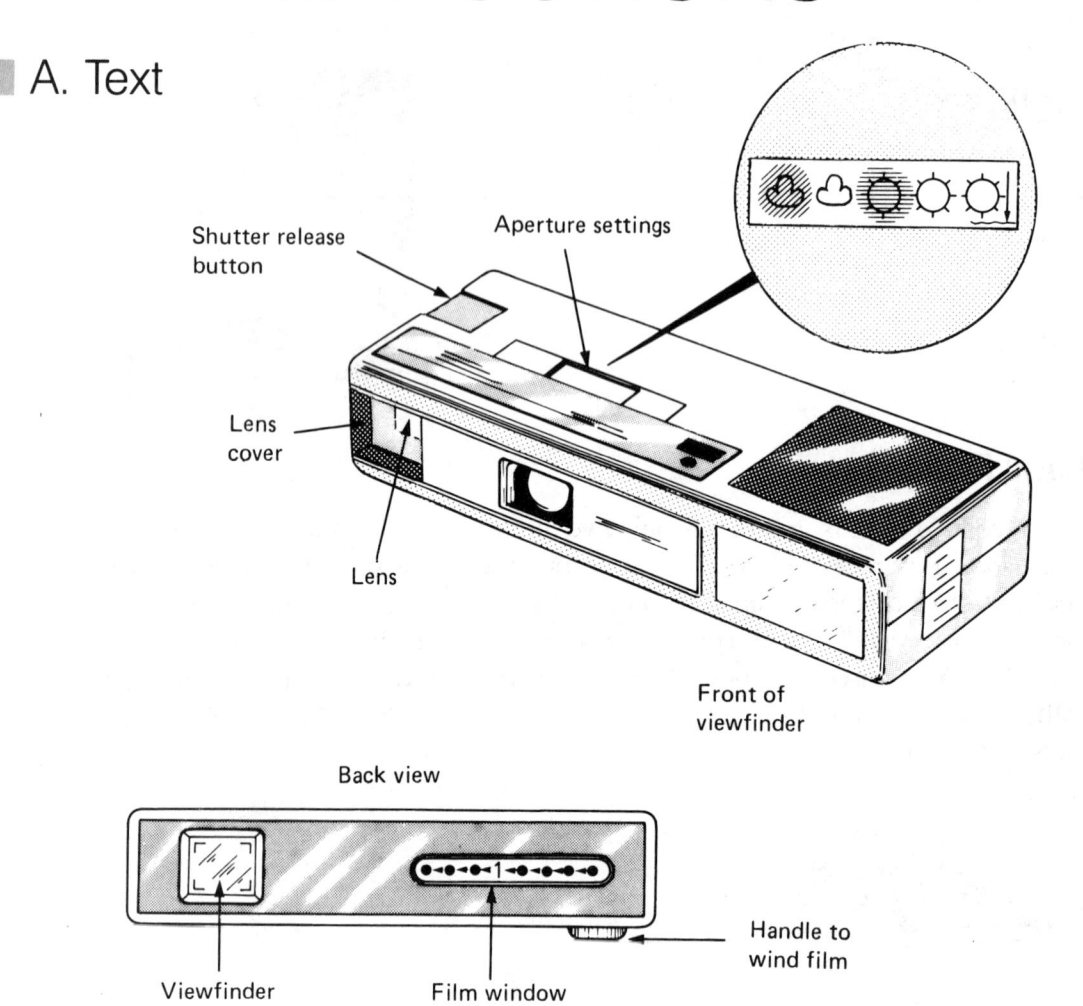

A. Text

Shutter release button
Aperture settings
Lens cover
Lens
Front of viewfinder

Back view

Viewfinder
Film window
Handle to wind film

In order to take photographs with your new Fotomatic 5, you must follow these simple instructions. First, take the film cassette out of its package and insert it into the back of the camera. Wind the film until a number 1 appears in the film window at the back of the camera.

Now set the aperture to one of the five positions, shown by the sun and cloud signs, according to the weather conditions. If it's a dark, cloudy day (not much light) set the aperture to the dark cloud position.

If it's a sunny day and you are near a pool or lake (lots of light) set the aperture to the sun-over-water position. Don't forget to take off the lens cover!

Look through the viewfinder and move the camera until what you want to photograph appears between the white lines. Hold the camera steady and press the shutter release button slowly. That's all you have to do to get perfect pictures!

B. Glossary

cassette	=	plastic box containing film
insert	=	put something into something else
wind the film	=	turn the handle that moves the film along
aperture	=	the hole that lets the light into the camera
lens	=	the glass in front of the aperture that collects the light
viewfinder	=	a small window in the camera that lets you see what you want to photograph
steady	=	firm, not moving
press	=	push
shutter	=	opens and closes the aperture to let light into the camera

C. Comprehension

1. What must you do first?
2. Where does the light enter the camera?
3. What do you look through when you take a photo?
4. Why are there different aperture positions?
5. What is the film kept in?

D. Analysis

1. Why do you think it's important to press the shutter release button slowly?
2. What do you think these five signs mean? They are used to show the different positions of the aperture.

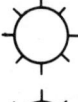

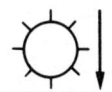

E. Discussion

1. Do you like to take pictures? Why?
2. Apart from vacations, in what situations might people take photographs?
3. Is it necessary to have a very expensive camera? Would it make your pictures turn out better?

F. Language Practice

1. Common Form

There are different ways of giving instructions. In the text, the most common form is used:

Take the film cassette out of the package.

The above form is often used in written instructions. When people give oral instructions, they often use the following form:

You take the film cassette out of the package.

Now rewrite these sentences in the same way:*

a. Insert the film into the camera.
b. Wind the film to number 1.
c. Set the aperture.
d. Take off the lens cover.
e. Look through the viewfinder.

2. Impersonal Form

If you want to be more impersonal, you can use this form:

The film cassette **should be taken out** of the package.

Now change sentences a – e above to look like this one.*

G. Writing Practice

1. Sequencing

Look at this picture. It shows a machine that sells soft drinks. The instructions for the machine are written below, but they are in the wrong order. Rewrite them in the correct sequence.*

Wait until the money drops.
Push the button to make a selection.
Deposit nickels, dimes or quarters.
If the can does not appear, press the *Coin Return* button.
Check the amount of money needed.

2. Sequencing Words

Some words are used to introduce sentences and show the correct sequence:

First, you take the film cassette out of its package, **and then** you insert it into the back of the camera.

After you take the film cassette out of its package, you insert it into the back of the camera.

Before you insert the film cassette into the back of the camera, you take it out of the package.

Finally, you wind the film until a number 1 appears in the film window.

Now look at the soft drink instructions again. Write a set of instructions and use sequencing words like those above to introduce the sentences. The first one is done for you.

First, you check the amount of money needed.

3. Impersonal Instructions

Read the friendly recipe below:

> "Well, hamburgers are really very simple. All you need is a pound of ground beef, which you mix with other things like salt, pepper, and paprika. Oh, and add an egg as well. Mix all the things together with a fork. When it's smooth and well-mixed, make round, flat hamburgers from the mixture. Then you need a frying pan and some oil. Fry the hamburgers for about 5 minutes on each side, until they're really brown. When they're ready, get some hamburger buns and put the hamburgers inside them. Oh, I forgot. First, spread the buns with mayonnaise and catsup. Put lettuce, tomatoes, and onions on top of the hamburgers and eat them as soon as possible."

Now rewrite this recipe in an impersonal way for a cookbook. First make a list of all the ingredients you need to use. Then make a list of the instructions in the correct order.

H. Writing Tasks

1. Write the ingredients for your favorite recipe, and then write the instructions to prepare the dish. Imagine it is for a magazine.

2. Imagine that a friend is going to stay in your house while you are away. You know that he or she wants to use your tape recorder and your washing machine. Choose ONE of these and write an informal note explaining how to use it. You will need to use words like these:

Tape Recorder
cassette	=	the container that holds the tape
play	=	the button that makes the tape run
reverse	=	the button that makes the tape run backward
fast forward	=	the button that makes the tape run forward at a high speed
eject	=	the button that opens the tape compartment and pushes the tape out
to record	=	to put the sounds on the tape
blank tape	=	tape with no sounds on it

Washing Machine
detergent	=	powder or liquid used to clean clothes
laundry	=	the clothes to be washed
to load	=	to put clothes into the machine
heat setting	=	the choice of cold, warm or hot water
water level	=	the choice of a small, medium or large amount of water
rotate	=	turn
clockwise	=	in the direction in which the hands of a clock move
counterclockwise	=	in the direction opposite to that which the hands of a clock move

3. Imagine that you are sending your favorite game to a friend. Explain how to play it in an informal letter. You may wish to draw pictures to help explain your instructions.

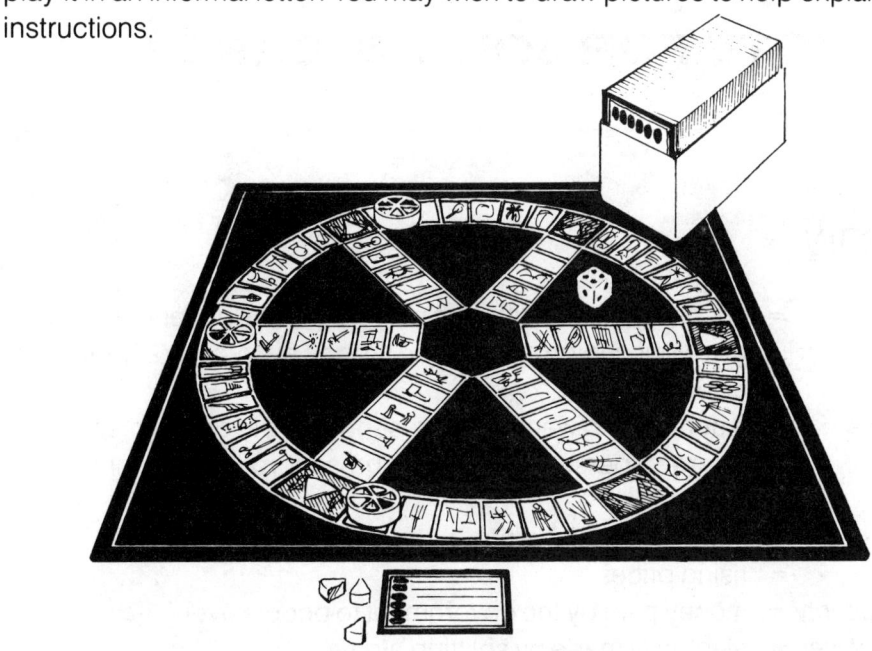

10. FUTURE PLANS

A. Text

> **VOTE FOR JOHN W. CASEY!**
>
> John W. Casey is the only candidate who is interested in helping everybody, not just small groups of his friends. John W. Casey has great plans for the future of this country, and this is what he will do if you elect him:
>
> ★ Reduce taxes, especially for low-income groups
> ★ Build more houses and help people to buy their own houses
> ★ Keep inflation as low as possible
> ★ Increase Social Security benefits
> ★ Fight crime in the cities
> ★ Stop the building of nuclear power plants
>
> **AMERICANS HAVE BUILT A GREAT COUNTRY.
> LET'S KEEP IT GREAT.**
>
> **VOTE FOR JOHN W. CASEY!**

B. Glossary

vote	= choose between different political parties or persons and give your choice at the same time as everybody else, in an election
candidate	= a person who wants to represent others in government
elect	= choose a person or party to represent you in government
reduce	= lower
income	= money that you earn
inflation	= rising prices
Social Security	= money paid by the government to people over 62
nuclear power	= electricity made by splitting atoms

C. Comprehension

1. What is different about John W. Casey – according to him?
2. How will he make life safer for everybody?
3. Who will gain most from the lower taxes?

D. Analysis

1. What groups of people is John W. Casey trying to attract most?
2. Why do you think he wants to stop the building of nuclear power plants?

E. Discussion

1. Do you think John W. Casey can fulfill all these promises?
2. Can you see any contradictions in his promises?

F. Language Practice

1. Intentions

There are different ways of expressing your plans or intentions, depending on how definite you are:

Definite intention	I'**m going to be** rich.
Not quite so definite	I'**m planning to go** away next week.
Less definite	I'**m hoping to visit** Scotland.
	I **hope to visit** Scotland.

Now rewrite John W. Casey's promises using each type of sentence above at least once.

Example: I'm going to reduce taxes.

2. Predictions

When talking about future events, you can't know what will happen, so you make a prediction. A prediction is what you think will happen:

I'm **sure** you know what you're doing. (definite)
I **think** you know what you're doing. (probable)
I **guess** you know what you're doing. (possible)

Now use two of each type of sentence to write what you think about John W. Casey's promises. Show what you believe he will or will not do.

Example: I think he's going to reduce taxes.

G. Writing Practice

1. Planning

When planning a schedule, you can use *could* to express possibility:

I **could leave** for Europe on Friday the 20th.

You work for a large computer company and they are sending you to a computer fair in Zurich, Switzerland. While you are there, they would like you to visit the university's computer center. You would also like to see a good friend who lives in town. This is your schedule:

Wednesday, March 9:	arrive Zurich 10:30 a.m.
Thursday, March 10:	computer fair begins 2:00 p.m.
Friday, March 11:	computer fair 8:00 a.m. - 6:00 p.m.
Saturday, March 12:	computer fair 8:00 a.m. - 12:00 p.m.
Sunday, March 13:	free day
Monday, March 14:	computer fair 8:00 a.m.- 6:00 p.m.
Tuesday, March 15:	computer fair 8:00 a.m. - 4:00 p.m.
	depart Zurich 10:00 p.m.

Use the schedule above to plan some possible times to visit the university and your friend. Begin your sentence with:

I could . . .

H. Writing Tasks

1. A friend is coming to visit you for a few days. Look at some advertisements from the entertainment section of your local paper. Then write a letter to him or her explaining what you both could do, what you would prefer, and asking what he or she would like to do.

2. You are a businessperson and have just found this note on your desk:

> November 23
>
> Dear Chris,
>
> We've got to get together as soon as possible to discuss our new advertising contract. I can stop by tomorrow, Friday or Monday afternoon. Let me know as soon as possible.
>
> If that's not good for you, maybe we could meet on the weekend.
>
> *Elliot*

Here is your calendar. Now write a note back to Elliot.

Monday 23rd

Tuesday 24th

Wednedsay 25th — Visit Syracuse office

Thursday 26th

Friday 27th — afternoon off

Saturday 28th — skiing

Sunday 29th — skiing

Monday 30th — 3:00 dentist

Tuesday 1st

Wednesday 2nd — 9:00 Board meeting

Thursday 3rd

Friday 4th

Saturday 5th

11. FORMAL LETTERS

A. Text

JOIN OUR WINNING SALES TEAM!

Alvan is a leading manufacturer of Mini Blinds, Window Shades and Vertical Drapes.

The candidate we are seeking will be energetic, ambitious and self-motivated and have a proven track record of accomplishments plus two years sales experience in the window treatment industry.

We offer an excellent salary, company car, expenses and company fringe benefits program.

Send your resume with salary history to:

AC

Allison Rockwood
Alvan Company
81 Forrest Drive
Chicago, IL 60040

B. Glossary

leading	=	big; makes more money than most other companies that make the same thing
energetic	=	lots of energy; ready to work hard
ambitious	=	wanting to do well
self-motivated	=	able to act without being told
proven track record	=	success at jobs in the past
company car	=	automobile owned by the company but used by the employee
expenses	=	repayment by the company for any money spent on travel, hotel, etc. while doing the job
fringe benefits program	=	advantages such as medical and dental insurance
salary history	=	the amount of money you were paid in past jobs

C. Comprehension

1. What kind of job is offered in this advertisement?
2. What kind of person should you be to do this job?
3. What kind of experience do you need to do this job?
4. What will you be selling?
5. What do you have to do to get an interview?

D. Analysis

1. Why do you think they are looking for the type of person described?
2. What do you think "window treatment industry" means?
3. Why do you think a company car and expenses are mentioned in the advertisement?

E. Discussion

1. Would you like this sort of job? Why or why not?
2. Name some jobs that could give you sales experience.

F. Language Practice

1. Formal Vocabulary

Some words are more formal than others, and are more often used in formal letters:

Informal	Formal
job	position
get	obtain
give	provide
terrific	excellent
need	require
want (to desire)	wish
someone	the applicant

Now rewrite the text below using formal words instead of informal ones:

This job offers a terrific salary, and gives a good opportunity for someone who wants to get experience. We need people who are enthusiastic and hard-working. Sales experience is preferred.

2. Introducing Sentences

When two sentences are joined together, you can make the first one more interesting in this way:

⎵I⎵ have seen your advertisement and ⎵I⎵ would like to apply for the job.

Having seen your advertisement, I would like to apply for the job.

⎵He⎵ worked in a bank and ⎵he⎵ understands business.

Having worked in a bank, he understands business.

Note: Use *having* + the past participle:
　　　having gone

Notice that the sentences you are joining above have the *same subject*.

Now change the following sentences in the same way:*

- **a.** I have learned Spanish and I want to visit South America.
- **b.** He failed his exams and he went back to school.
- **c.** She took the Civil Service test and she went for an interview.
- **d.** He taught in a school and he knows a lot about children.

G. Writing Practice

1. Beginning and Ending a Formal Letter

Formal letters usually look a little different from informal letters (see Unit 1). Three things are usually added to formal letters:

- your own address
- the address of the person you are writing to
- your own name typed under the signature

Now look at the example on the following page:

```
                        150 West 43rd St.
                        Pittsburgh, Pennsylvania  15601
                        November 6, 1987


General Manager
Collins Hotel
15950 Sand Street
Boulder, Colorado  80053

Dear Sir or Madam:




                        Sincerely,


                        Jack Barratt
```

Look at the greeting in the letter. You can use:

Dear Sir or Madam — if you don't know who the person is
Dear Sir — if you know the person is a man but you don't know his name
Dear Madam — if you know the person is a woman but you don't know her name

If you know the person's name, you can start with:

Dear Ms. Smith — if you don't know whether she's married
Dear Mrs. Smith — if she is married
Dear Miss Smith — if she is not married
Dear Mr. Smith

You can end these letters with **Sincerely** or **Sincerely yours.**

Now practice beginning and ending letters to the following people. Remember to start with the person's name if you know it.

   a. General Manager, City Bank, 29 Main Street, Hillsboro, OR 97017
   b. Arlene Baker, Con Edison, 115 West 54th Street, New York, NY 20202
   c. Joe Caruso, Principal, Central High School, 60 North Parkway, Kittyhawk, SC 29204

2. Making Requests

Often when you write a formal letter, you want someone to do something for you. You must make this request in a formal way. Here are some examples:

Formal: I'd be very grateful if you would . . .
Formal: I wonder if you could possibly . . .
Less formal: Do you think you could . . . ?
Informal: Could you . . . ?

Now use the phrases above, and the letter beginnings and endings, to write short letters to the following places:

1. Ask for a travel brochure from the Tourist Office, 11 Magnolia Ave., Greensboro, NC 27604.
2. Ask American Language Vacations, Inc. (see Unit 2) to send your evaluation to the Admissions Office, University of Washington, Seattle, WA 95412.

H. Writing Tasks

1. Look at this advertisement for a job. Write a letter to apply for it.

> **BANK TELLERS**
> For large bank. 15 trainees, 12 experienced.
> Work in Bronx, Manh, Bklyn, Queens, Yonkers.
> To $250/wk. Write:
> 　　　　Personnel Manager
> 　　　　P.O. Box 717Q
> 　　　　New York, NY 10017

2. Write a formal letter to a department store where you bought slippers while you were on vacation. Explain that the slippers fell apart and ask the store to replace them, or to return your money – $12.99.

3. Write a letter to the manager of your bank explaining that you are going to study in Britain for a year. Ask the bank to transfer $500 a month from your checking account (#9963214) to the Bank of Scotland, 17 Princes St., Edinburgh.

4. Look at this advertisement for a leather chair. You would like to buy it, but you want more information. You want to know how big it is, what colors the leather comes in, and how long it would take to deliver. Write a letter asking these questions and any other information you think you need.

LEATHER CHAIR

Leather luxury is combined with the ultimate in comfort! Available in over 20 colors of top quality leather.

Style AZ42 . . . $827.00
Shipping charges extra.

Write for our free catalog.

Southwest Leathers, Inc.
P.O. Box 0264X
Cedars, OR 97771
(503) 555-1999

12. REPORTING

A. Text

These are the notes made by a police officer at the scene of an accident. Read them carefully and then answer the questions. Some of the words are explained on the next page.

```
11:08  Emergency call — accident on Highway 101 between Burlingame and
         San Mateo
       2 cars and 1 truck involved
11:09  Requested ambulance and fire engine
11:10  Left police station in car with Officer Lakey
11:17  Arrived at scene of accident
       Ambulance and fire engine already arrived
       Situation: Collision between truck going north, gray car following,
         and white car coming south
       Casualties:  1 person killed (in white Ford)
                    2 people injured (one trapped, in gray Toyota)
                    1 truck driver slightly injured
       Road conditions: Wet and slippery
       Cause:  Front left tire of truck had a blowout. Truck skidded across
         the road.
11:19  Second ambulance arrived. First ambulance left with one injured and
       one dead person.
       Action: Directed traffic
               Radioed for photographer and tow truck
               Officer Lakey spoke to people involved (see Interview Form)
               Officer Lakey filled out Accident Report Form
11:26  Trapped person was freed and left in second ambulance
11:30  Officer Lakey completed chalk marks on road
       Police photographer arrived
11:45  Tow truck arrived to clear road
12:00  Road clear
       Returned to station
```

B. Glossary

emergency	=	serious or dangerous situation
collision	=	crash; vehicles violently hitting each other
casualties	=	people killed or hurt
trapped	=	kept from moving; not able to get out of something
slightly	=	a little; not much
slippery	=	smooth; difficult to stand or move on
blowout	=	a hole blown in a tire
skid	=	slipping movement of the wheels of a car moving at high speed
tow truck	=	vehicle with equipment for pulling cars that have broken down
freed	=	set loose from something that holds one back
chalk marks	=	marks made with chalk to show where vehicles hit each other

C. Comprehension

1. Where did the accident happen?
2. How many people were injured?
3. In which car was one person killed?
4. What were the road conditions like?
5. In which direction was the truck traveling?
6. What was the cause of the accident?

D. Analysis

Look at this drawing of the accident, and then answer the questions.

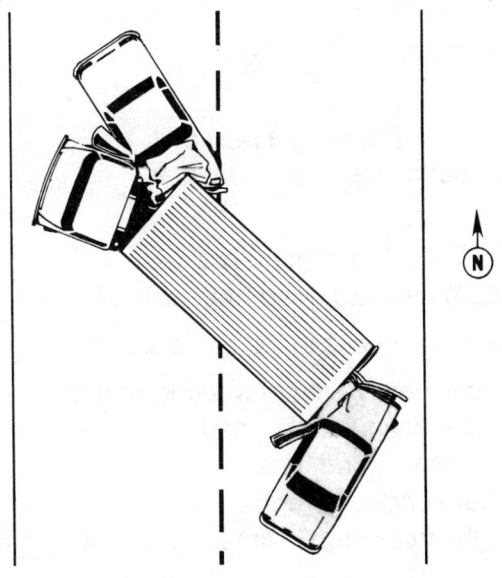

1. Which vehicle caused the accident?
2. Which car probably hit the truck first?
3. Why do you think the gray car couldn't stop in time?
4. Why do you think the gray car is in the middle of the road?
5. Why do you think the white car crashed harder than the gray car?

Some information is not given in the text, but from the situation and the information that is given, you can work it out. If you are not sure, explain what probably happened.

6. How many people went to the hospital in the first ambulance?
7. Who freed the trapped person from the gray car?
8. Why did the police officer make chalk marks on the road?

E. Discussion

1. What do you think could have prevented the accident?
2. How should people drive under wet and slippery road conditions?
3. Highway 101 is a narrow road. Should trucks be allowed to drive on narrow roads?

F. Language Practice

Look at this example:

He | was | driving fast.
He | **shouldn't have been** | driving fast.

Now change these sentences in the same way:*

a. He was following the truck very closely.
b. He was looking out of the side window.
c. He was driving without a seat belt.

Look at these examples:

He | wasn't | wearing a seat belt.
He | **should have been** | wearing a seat belt.

The truck | didn't | have good brakes.
The truck | **should have** | had good brakes.

Now change these sentences in the same way:*

d. The windshield wipers were not working properly.
e. He wasn't concentrating on the road.
f. The truck didn't have good tires.
g. He wasn't driving under 40 mph.
h. He didn't see the truck stop in time.

G. Writing Practice

1. Sequencing

These sentences describe what happened on Highway 101, but they are not in the correct order. Rewrite them in the order that they happened.*

   a. The driver was killed immediately.
   b. It had a blowout.
   c. The road was blocked for an hour.
   d. A gray Toyota traveling north also hit the truck.
   e. It skidded across the road.
   f. A truck was driving north.
   g. A white Ford traveling south hit the truck.

2. Linking

Look at this example:

The police officer directed the traffic. The workers from the ambulance helped the injured people.

The police officer directed the traffic **while** the workers from the ambulance helped the injured people.

Now join these sentences in the same way:

   a. The photographer took pictures.
      The police officer made chalk marks on the road.
   b. Officer Lakey spoke to Mrs. Smith.
      The other police officer radioed for a tow truck.
   c. The second ambulance arrived.
      The fire fighters freed Mr. Smith from his car.
   d. The police officer wrote her report.
      The tow truck cleared the road.

3. Reporting What People Say

When you write down what someone has said to you, you must change the form of the sentence. Look at this example:

John said, " | I saw | an accident on Saturday."
John said | **he had seen** | an accident on Saturday.

Now read what the two drivers, Mr. Smith and Mr. Kowalski, had to say about the accident.

Mr. Smith said, "I heard a loud bang and then saw the truck skid across the road. I don't remember anything else after that."

Mr. Kowalski said, "I heard a loud bang and felt the truck start to skid. I think the wheels stopped turning. I don't know what happened after that."

Police officers have to fill out Interview Forms after an accident. They report what people have said to them. Make your own form and report what Mr. Smith and Mr. Kowalski said.*

```
Interview Form
Name: _____
Time: _____
Statement: _____
_____
_____
_____
_____
```

4. Writing Reports

   a. The police officer who was at the scene of the accident has to rewrite her notes as a report, using full sentences and writing in a formal, impersonal way. For example:

   11:08 Emergency call – accident on Highway 101 between Burlingame and San Mateo, 2 cars and 1 truck involved

   A report would be written this way:

   At 11:08, there was an emergency call. The caller said that there had been an accident on Highway 101 between Burlingame and San Mateo. There were two cars and one truck involved in the accident.

   Now practice writing in this way, and finish the police officer's report for her.

   b. The notes below were written by a newspaper reporter sitting in a courtroom listening to a murder trial. Write a short report from the following facts:

   Dan Lane / 35 / killed wife / found her with his best friend / been having an affair for two years / Lane couldn't stop himself / hit her with hammer / very unhappy in court / judge sentenced him to ten years in jail

H. Writing Tasks

1. Magda Smith, Mr. Smith's wife, wrote a letter to her mother describing what happened (see exercise G3). Here is the beginning and end of the letter. Now write the rest of it.

> Dear Mom,
> Something terrible happened yesterday...
>
> Love,
> Magda

2. Imagine you are a fire fighter returning from a serious fire in a supermarket. Write a report of what happened.

3. Imagine you are a reporter from the local radio station. Write a report describing what happened when someone famous came to visit the town. Pick your own famous person. Make the report serious.

13. SUMMARIZING

A. Text

'I couldn't let it go into the archives'
'Oldest' man only 104 years old

Canadian Press

NORTHBROOK, Ont.

David Trumble, who said he was 118 and the world's oldest person, was in fact 104, says one of his sons.

"I couldn't let it go into the archives," Clayton Trumble, 70, said during his father's funeral on Tuesday in this hamlet 50 kilometres north of Belleville. "I owe it to the other people who are as old and have the documents to back it up."

He said his father's marriage certificate lists David Trumble as 30 in 1912.

He said his oldest brother, Versy, who is on vacation in the United States, is 73. "Just add 73 and 30 (plus nine months to have a son) and that would make my father 104."

An unsuccessful attempt was made last February to enter Mr. Trumble in the Guinness Book of World Records as the world's oldest human being. A British woman, 112, now holds that honor after the death of a 120-year-old Japanese man.

Mr. Trumble was refused the record because he had no birth certificate to support his claim.

At least four other members of the immediate Trumble family supported Clayton Trumble's claim that David Trumble was younger than 118.

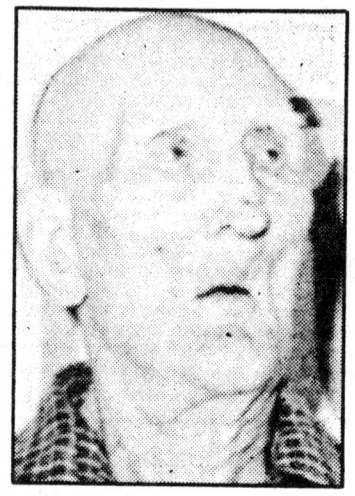

David Trumble

Step-great-grandson David Todd of Consecon, Ont., said his great-grandfather told him he was 109 when he visited him in a Belleville hospital last week.

Another Trumble daughter, Edna Todd, said she had seen a Bible with her father's birth date, which she thought was Dec. 15, 1883. That would have made him 103.

Clayton Trumble said his father added 11 years to his life when he accepted a 1967 centennial award from Pierre Trudeau, then prime minister. He said Mr. Trudeau's office accepted the claim, apparently without checking the data.

The award plus the taping of two books on his life, When I was a Boy, published in 1976, and The Road to St. Ola, in 1978, reinforced his claim in the public mind.

The books also gave him a reputation as a gifted storyteller.

He recalled with gusto his brawling days in the lumber camps north of Belleville, his experiences in the trenches during the First World War, his short-lived police career in nearby Picton, and his job as a midway boss.

If you doubted the authenticity of his tales about sleeping with the bears, his reputation as an iron man, his ability as a champion trapper, axeman, shooter and rider, David Trumble had a ready answer.

"That's true," he would say. "If it is not true, where are you going to find a witness?"

The witness now is Clayton Trumble, who says he has no axe to grind by revealing the truth about the age of his father, who outlived four wives and 14 of his 19 children.

He said he worried about the family's good name, adding that it was enough that his father lived to be more than 100 and was well-liked in the community.

At Tuesday's funeral, the Pentacostal Church was jammed during the hour-long ceremony.

B. Glossary

archives	=	records of past events
funeral	=	a formal gathering held for a dead person before burying him or her
hamlet	=	small village
50 kilometers	=	about 30 miles
documents	=	papers that show proof
certificate	=	a paper that contains information shown to be true
Guinness Book of World Records	=	book that shows the largest, tallest, heaviest, oldest, etc.
claim	=	something a person says is true but cannot prove
immediate family	=	a wife, a husband, and their children
step-great-grandson	=	a great-grandson who is part of the family through remarriage
centennial	=	celebration of 100 years
prime minister	=	the official head of a parliamentary government
data	=	facts
taping	=	recording on tape
reinforced	=	strengthened
reputation	=	known by others to have a certain ability
gusto	=	enthusiasm, excitement
brawling	=	fighting
trenches	=	ditches
short-lived	=	lasting a short time
midway	=	the part of a fair where there are amusements and food
authenticity	=	truth
champion	=	winner of first prize in competition
trapper	=	someone who traps animals for their fur
axeman	=	someone who uses an axe
witness	=	someone who saw an event and gives proof that it happened
"axe to grind"	=	a personal reason for disagreement or complaint
jammed	=	very crowded

C. Comprehension

1. What was David Trumble's real age according to his son?
2. How much older did he claim to be?
3. Who is the world's oldest human being?
4. How many wives and children did David Trumble have?
5. Why didn't *The Guinness Book of World Records* accept his claim?

D. Analysis

1. What information did David Trumble's children give that showed he was less than 118? List the facts.
2. What kind of experiences did his stories describe?
3. Why are quotation marks used in the headline?

E. Discussion

1. What kind of person was David Trumble, in your opinion?
2. What kind of person is Clayton Trumble, in your opinion?
3. Why do you think people were willing to accept the false story?

F. Language Practice

1. Embedding

To combine sentences and make them more concise, you can put one inside the other:

Marianne Gullaksen is not at work today.
Her sister came to visit.

Marianne Gullaksen, **whose sister came to visit,** is not at work today.

Now join these sentences in the same way:*

a. Henry Fonda received an Oscar for his role in the movie "On Golden Pond."
   His acting career lasted many years.
b. Boy George has just made another hit record.
   His hair is now a different color.
c. The Grassy Narrows Indians have complained to the government.
   Their fish are being poisoned.
d. The Blue Jays are playing good baseball again.
   Their record last year was very good.
e. Angie DiBianco is now recovering in the hospital.
   Her friend saved her from drowning.

2. Headlines

Headlines are sometimes like notes. They are short versions of sentences with some words missing. This is an example of *telegraphic* language. Look at the headline in the text. Can you guess which words are missing?

The sentence should be:

The 'oldest' man **is** only 104 years old.

So the missing words are *the* and *is*.

Others that are often missed are *a, his, her, their, was, were, has, have, has been, have been*.

Now rewrite these headlines as complete sentences:*

a. Workers warned today about strike
b. New taxes recently introduced by government
c. Ten people killed yesterday in car crash
d. Prince engaged to childhood friend
e. Pope's visit to synagogue great success

G. Writing Practice

1. Making Notes

The first step in summarizing, whether it is a lecture or a story, is to make notes about the facts. For example, the story about Mr. Trumble contains much more than the necessary facts. So the first thing to do is to write down the main points in telegraphic language:

David Trumble, who said he was 118 and the world's oldest person, was in fact 104, says one of his sons.

– Claims to be world's oldest person
– Son says claim not true
– 104, not 118

Now make notes about the other facts in the same way.

2. Writing a Summary

The next step is to make complete sentences from the notes you have just made and then combine them in different ways. One way could be:

The son of a man who claimed to be 118, the world's oldest person, says that he was really 104.

Now give the rest of the details about the story by using the other facts you have listed. Join them together to form complete sentences. Remember that your summary should be much shorter than the article in Section A.

3. Condensing

Another way to make your writing more concise is to take out unnecessary adjectives:

> **Attractive** mother of two Mrs. Stella Jones became the **proud** owner of a **lovely, new** dishwasher after winning an **exciting** competition at the opening of Wallbaum's **huge downtown** supermarket.

This report is 30 words long. If you take out the adjectives, it is only 23 words long.

Another way to make writing more concise is to take out unnecessary information such as age, physical description, and facts that don't add a lot to our understanding of what happened. Look at this example:

> "I couldn't let it go into the archives," Clayton Trumble, **70,** said **during his father's funeral on Tuesday in this hamlet 50 kilometers north of Belleville.** "I owe it to the other people who are as old and have the documents to back it up."

By taking out the words shown, the text is reduced from 45 words to 29 words. Now practice this by shortening the story below.

The Big Storm Is Pummeling Rockies Now

Denver

The last of the Pacific storms that caused the worst flooding in years in California and Nevada blew into the Rockies, dumping up to three feet of snow in Colorado.

The storms caused flooding in Utah and Colorado and strained dams to the breaking point.

Utah Governor Norm Bangerter declared Cache, Wasatch, Weber and Morgan counties as flood disaster areas, saying the counties no longer had the ability to fight the heavy storm.

Snow fell from Wyoming and Colorado to South Dakota. In northwest Colorado, the storm dropped 15 inches of heavy, wet snow on top of frozen rain, causing dangerous driving conditions and breaking power lines and cutting telephone service.

Up to three feet of snow fell at Rabbit Ears Pass, Colorado, and 13 inches covered Winter Park. Snowslides killed one person in Wyoming and two in Utah.

Winds 25 to 50 miles an hour blew across northeast Montana and western North Dakota. It was 35 below zero at Wolf Point, Montana, the lowest temperature reading in the nation.

The bitter cold moved south as far as Texas, taking the place of record high temperatures. Goodland, Kansas reported a record high of 75 degrees on Wednesday. It was 14 degrees and snowing there yesterday.

Heavy fog covered much of the nation east of the Mississippi River.

United Press Int'l 1986

Note: 75°F = 24 °C
50 mph = 80 kilometers per hour

H. Writing Tasks

1. Imagine you work for the tourist office in your hometown. You are asked to write a brief history of your town.
2. Write a brief life story of a famous person from your country.
3. Bring in your own newspaper story and summarize it to about one-third of its original length.
4. This description of orange farming in Florida is about 460 words long. Prepare two summaries of it:
   a. the bare facts (40-50 words)
   b. a summary of 150 words

ORANGE FARMING IN FLORIDA

A freshly squeezed glass of orange juice is a favorite drink on the breakfast table. If squeezing takes too long, frozen juice from Florida is the next best thing. Mix with water and serve! Florida's golden sunshine is there in every sip.

The United States grows about forty percent of the world's oranges. Florida grows about sixty percent of the U.S. crop and California grows most of the rest.

Because Florida gets more rain than other orange-farming areas, it produces extra juicy oranges. This makes them especially good for squeezing and for making into concentrate, which is then frozen.

Oranges originally came from Asia. They were then brought to Spain by the Arabs. Spanish settlers carried them to Florida about 400 years ago. The Florida Indians liked them and started to grow oranges themselves.

A warm climate is, of course, necessary to grow oranges. But if there is a lot of sunshine and warmth, the oranges tend to dry out a little. It is better not to grow them in southern Florida. On the other hand, if they grow too far north, they might be killed by cruel frosts. The middle part of the state is the best place for oranges to grow.

Orange trees are planted on gently sloping land so that water drains downhill. Even more important, cool air flows downhill too. Cold, frosty air collects in a "pool" in the valley below, and leaves the orange groves safe in the soft, mild air.

Another thing that orange growers often do in order to protect their precious trees is to plant rows of tall trees all around the grove, especially on the north side. These rows of tall trees are called windbreaks, and they help to break the force of any cold winds that might blow.

When the oranges are ready for harvesting, two machines are used. The first machine moves along between the rows, taking each tree in turn around the trunk and shaking it firmly. The second machine moves along behind the first, scooping all the oranges off the ground. The best oranges are put into trucks and delivered to the orange juice factories. Any damaged oranges, or any that are not ripe enough for juice, are taken out to be fed to cattle.

The orange growing business is not easy. Farmers know that they may sometimes lose a crop because of serious frost damage. They do many things to protect their crops. They try to arrange the crops so that the oranges do not all ripen at the same time. As many as twenty-eight different varieties of oranges are grown, ripening at different times of the year. Also, the trees are arranged so that different groves ripen at different times. This allows a steady stream of oranges to be available at most times of the year – all ready to give us that glass of Florida sunshine even when snow is on the ground, or the cold winds of March whistle through northern lands.

14. ADVISING & WARNING

A. Text

YOU ARE WHAT YOU EAT!

YOU SHOULD CHECK THAT YOUR DIET CONTAINS THE ESSENTIAL VITAMINS.

EAT RIGHT!

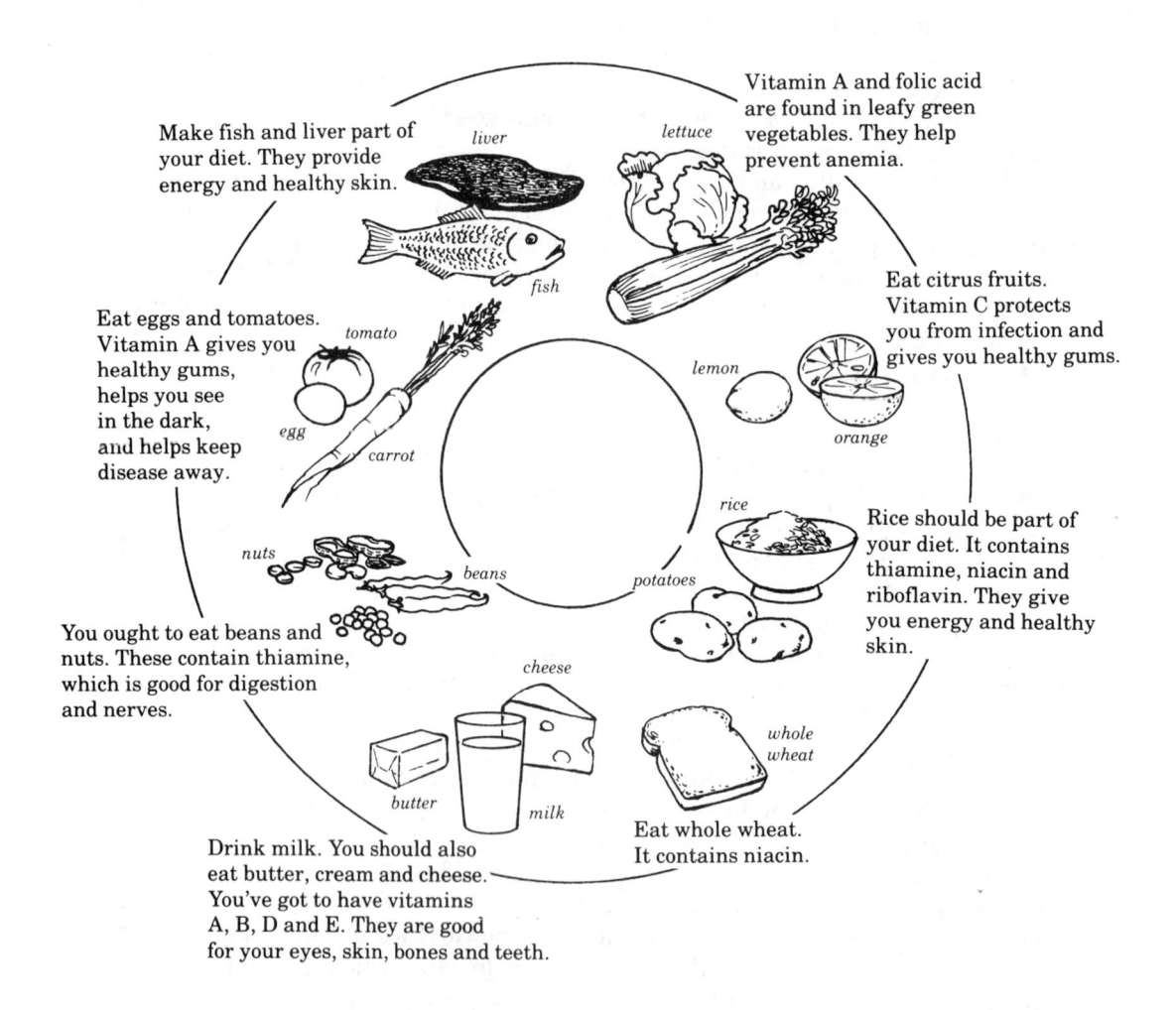

Make fish and liver part of your diet. They provide energy and healthy skin.

Vitamin A and folic acid are found in leafy green vegetables. They help prevent anemia.

Eat citrus fruits. Vitamin C protects you from infection and gives you healthy gums.

Eat eggs and tomatoes. Vitamin A gives you healthy gums, helps you see in the dark, and helps keep disease away.

Rice should be part of your diet. It contains thiamine, niacin and riboflavin. They give you energy and healthy skin.

You ought to eat beans and nuts. These contain thiamine, which is good for digestion and nerves.

Eat whole wheat. It contains niacin.

Drink milk. You should also eat butter, cream and cheese. You've got to have vitamins A, B, D and E. They are good for your eyes, skin, bones and teeth.

B. Glossary

essential = necessary
gums = pink tissue that covers part of the teeth
thiamine = vitamin B$_1$
digestion = how the body breaks down food to use for energy
niacin = vitamin B group
riboflavin = vitamin B$_2$
infection = the spread of disease
leafy = having many leaves
prevent = to keep from happening
anemia = not enough iron in the blood
deficiency = lack, not enough of

C. Comprehension

1. Which foods provide energy?
2. Which foods keep your skin healthy?
3. Which foods protect you from infectious diseases?
4. Which foods help your eyesight?
5. What are citrus fruits?

D. Analysis

1. What would be a good balanced diet for one day?

E. Discussion

1. How might different beliefs affect the advice given in the text?
2. Do you think your present diet is a healthy one? Can you think of ways to improve it?

F. Language Practice

1. Giving Advice

Here are some examples of giving advice:

If you want to pass your driving test, you **ought to take** lessons.
you **should take** lessons.
you **have to take** lessons.
you**'ve got to take** lessons.
take lessons.

Note: 've is a contraction for *have*

Now make sentences in the same way from these words:*

   a. If you / go to college / work hard
   b. If he / work in the USA / get work permit first
   c. If you / be successful / get up early
   d. If they / make a lot of money / start their own business

Here are some more examples:

If I were you, **I'd do** this.
            I'd advise you to do this.

Practice giving advice to someone who wants to
- be rich.
- be more beautiful.
- be famous.
- live a long life.

2. Making Suggestions

If someone has a problem, your advice might include a suggested solution to the problem:

I don't feel well.
  1. **Go** to a doctor.
  2. You **should go** to a doctor.
  3. **Why don't you go** to a doctor?
  4. You **could go** to a doctor.

The numbers show a scale of advice / suggestion. Numbers 1 and 2 are strong suggestions, while 3 and 4 are not as strong.

Your friends have lots of problems. Write strong or weak suggestions to solve these problems. Begin your sentences with *You*.*

   a. He is overweight.
   b. She never has enough money to pay her bills.
   c. His apartment is always very cold.
   d. Her car never starts in the morning.

G. Writing Practice

1. Warning

As well as giving advice, you often have to warn people when they are doing something dangerous or wrong. You can use sentences like:

   Be careful not to do that. It could be dangerous.
   You **shouldn't do** that. It's dangerous.
   Don't do that. It's dangerous.

Use the same forms to give advice or a warning about safety in the kitchen. Add to the list of Dos and Don'ts below. Give reasons to support your advice and warnings.

Dos	Don'ts
Keep the kitchen clean.	Don't wax the floor.
Keep cleaning liquids away from children.	Don't leave water on the floor.
Put wall cabinets low enough to reach.	Don't let children play with the stove.
Have a fire extinguisher ready.	Don't leave hot oil in a pot when you go out.

2. Analyzing

You can't give advice until you know what the problem is. You must analyze the parts of the problem and make a list of them so you can answer them.

Look at this problem letter from a newspaper:

> Dear Aunt Helpful,
>
> I'm so worried about my boyfriend that I can't sleep at night. I'm sure he still thinks a lot about his last girlfriend. She left him about six months ago, and he's still in love with her. He is unhappy if anyone says her name and I think he wants to take her out again. I'm unhappy because he won't take me out in the evenings. He says he is saving money. And now he tells me he will never marry anyone but this girl. What should I do? I still like him a lot.
>
> Julia

What are the different problems of the boy and girl? Make two lists:

Boy's problems	Girl's problems
1. His last girlfriend left him.	1. He won't marry her.
2. _____	2. _____
3. _____	3. _____

Now write a letter to the girl giving advice on each of the problems.

H. Writing Tasks

1. You have just received this letter from a friend who always seems to be in trouble. Write a reply pointing out the problems and giving advice on them.

> I'm in a terrible mess. I've just lost my job because I had an argument with the boss. He wanted me to work on the weekend but I wanted to go to the city. I told him he was crazy to ask me to work on Saturday and he fired me!
>
> On top of that, the car broke down on the way home from work. I forgot to put water in the radiator. My girlfriend was very angry about it, and I said she was an idiot who knew nothing about cars. She said she didn't want to see me ever again.
>
> What'll I do? I have to get another job soon because I've got to pay the bills.
>
> Yours, Sandy

2. You have an American friend who wants to go to your country to live and work. Write a letter giving advice on what he or she should do to get a job, and what he or she needs to know to live happily in your country. (120-150 words)
3. You have been asked to write a short article for your school newspaper suggesting interesting places to visit in your area. Write strong suggestions about places that should not be missed and weaker suggestions about less important places.

15. PERSUADING

A. Text

THE GOLD STAR BREAKFAST

There's nothing wrong with champagne at breakfast time. In fact, it's a very refreshing start to the day. Champagne, however, is a little more expensive these days. So it's a comforting thought for our passengers to know that beautifully chilled French champagne is theirs for the asking, at any time of day or night.

It's all part of our Gold Star Service for business people on long distance flights – and it costs no more than economy class travel. But with free champagne, how can we call it economy class?

B. Glossary

refreshing	=	restoring energy; reviving
champagne	=	sparkling wine
comforting	=	makes you feel better
chilled	=	cooled quite a bit but not frozen
theirs for the asking	=	free
economy class	=	the cheapest way to fly

C. Comprehension

1. What is this advertisement trying to sell?
2. What is Gold Star Service?
3. Why do writers of the advertisement think it is wrong to call their normal service "economy"?
4. Does Gold Star Service cost more?

D. Analysis

1. The passenger in the advertisement is wearing pajamas. What effect does this have? What do you think when you see it?
2. Why do you think the airline wants to show its passengers like this?
3. Apart from pajamas, what else is casual or unusual about the picture of the passenger?
4. Champagne is very expensive. Why do you think this airline gives it away free?

E. Discussion

1. Do you think offering alcoholic drinks is an acceptable way to get people to fly on airlines?
2. If you were flying somewhere, would you prefer free champagne or a cheaper ticket?

F. Language Practice

1. Suggesting

The first step in getting someone to do or buy something is to make a suggestion:

We **suggest you travel** to Jamaica. (formal)
Why don't you travel to Jamaica?
How about traveling to Jamaica?
Why not travel to Jamaica?
Let's go to Jamaica.

Now practice making suggestions from these words:*

a. we / have / dinner party (informal)
b. camping / Colorado (informal)
c. try / Ladle Soup (informal)
d. I / we meet / discuss business (formal)
e. you / buy / new TV

2. Persuading

The suggestions you've just made may not be strong enough to convince someone. Then you need to persuade. Here are some ways to persuade people:

You'll really enjoy seeing the White House.
You've got to see the White House.
You really should see the White House.
Don't you think you should see the White House?
Maybe you should see the White House. It's fantastic.

Another way is to exaggerate the qualities of the thing you are describing. Use words like:

amazing	**fantastic**
incredible	**excellent**
wonderful	**terrific**
unbelievable	

Now practice persuading by writing sentences about the following:*

a. camping
b. going on a diet
c. buying a new record
d. learning to play the piano
e. buying a new VCR

G. Writing Practice

1. Emphasizing Quality

In order to persuade people, you often need to stress how good something is:

It's **really** good.
It's **very** reliable.
It's made of the **highest quality** materials.
Tennis is **excellent** exercise and a lot of fun.

Use some of these words to persuade people to:

a. go mountain climbing
b. buy a motorcycle
c. try a new dessert

2. Advertisements

Advertisements usually try to persuade you to buy an object or a service. To do this, they often:

- suggest the product will make you happy.
- suggest the product will save you money.

- claim it is the best product you can buy
- suggest something bad may happen if you don't buy it
- suggest you will be more popular if you do buy it

Now look at this advertisement and describe what it is persuading you to do.

THE COLOR OF LIFE

ANNOUNCING THE MOST ACCURATE, REALISTIC COLOR IN PRINT FILM.

Kodacolor VR-G 100

NEW KODACOLOR VR-G
THE COLOR OF LIFE

Reprinted courtesy of Eastman Kodak Company

3. Giving Reasons

Here are some ways of explaining why one thing is better than another:

This car is better **because of** its reliability.
This car is better **because** it's reliable.
More people are traveling by train **because of** the price.
The reason for the concert is to raise money for world hunger.

Use the above phrases to expand these notes on the imaginary country of Greatland. They explain why Greatland would be a very good place to live. Write a short text giving all the reasons:

<u>Greatland</u>
- below-average divorce rate
- above-average number of cars
- large number of TVs
- lowest population density of industrial countries
- high number of students at universities
- low suicide rate

H. Writing Tasks

1. Look at this advertisement and then write a description explaining:

who is being persuaded, what it is persuading them to do or think, and how it is successful.

2. Your cousin has written to you explaining that he wants to leave his wife and family and live with someone else. Write to him to try to persuade him not to do it. Give a lot of reasons.

3. You have received a letter from your employer explaining that the company wants to save money so they are firing fifty people. You are one of them. Write a reply persuading him to change his mind. Give reasons.

16. DESCRIBING PROCESSES

A. Text

MAKING A RECORD

There are many different steps in the making of a record. Here is a description of the process that brings records into the stores.

1. The musicians play and sing. The sound they make is picked up by the microphones (about 24-30 of them).

2. The sounds are changed into electricity and sent through wires to the mixer, where they are made louder or quieter.

3. The signals are then sent to the tape recorder, which records them onto 24 tracks on the tape. All the instruments are kept separate.

4. Then the recordings are mixed again, and a new tape is made with only two tracks (stereo). Some sounds are placed on the "left" of the tape so they can be heard from the left loudspeaker.

5. This stereo tape is taken to the cutting machine. This machine cuts a groove into a piece of metal. Two pieces of metal are cut – one for Side One and one for Side Two of the record.

6. This metal disc with grooves is then used to make another metal disc – with ridges. The new disc is called a master.

7. From the master, a steel disc with grooves is made. This is called a mother. It is played by engineers who check the sound quality.

8. From the mother, two son discs or stampers are made. The son discs are put into a pressing machine with some black plastic or vinyl in the middle.

9. The press is heated and the plastic melts and flows between the ridges of the metal discs. So a plastic record is made, with grooves cut into each of its sides. This is cooled with water and taken out.

10. The record is put into a sleeve and then into a jacket and sent to the record store.

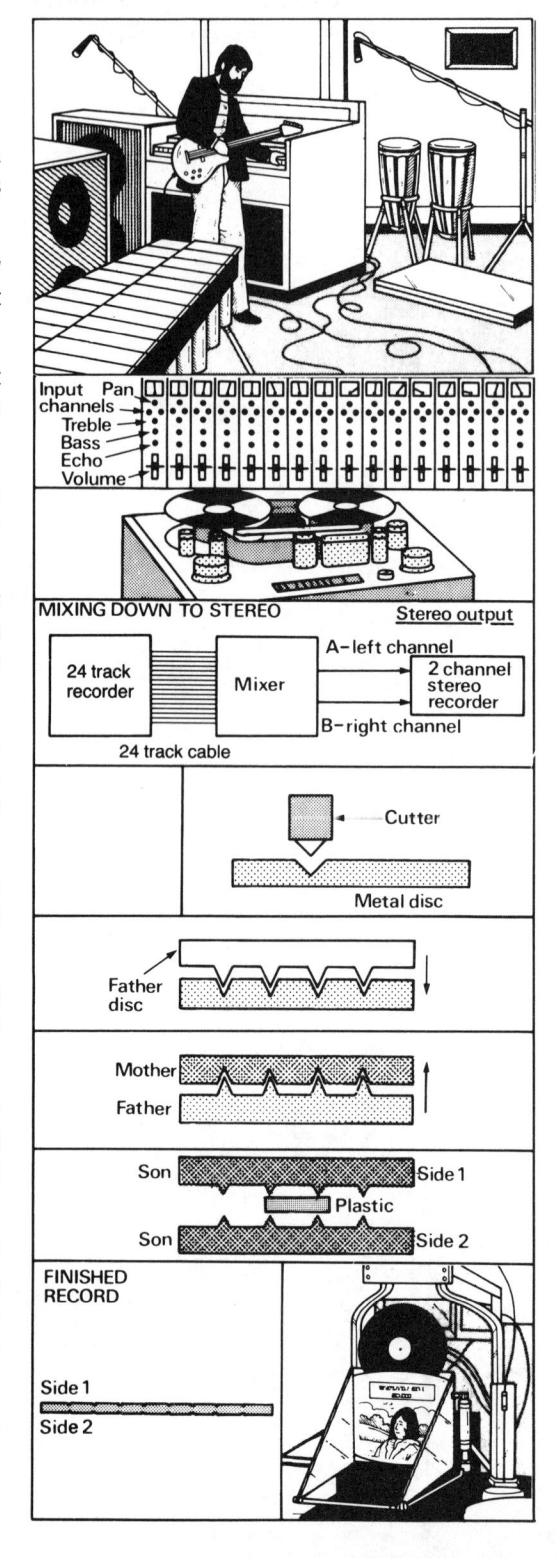

B. Glossary

process	=	a way of doing things
wires	=	thin metal lines that carry electric current – usually wrapped in rubber
mixer	=	a machine that balances and controls sound
signal	=	sound that has been changed into electricity
tracks	=	side-by-side paths on a magnetic tape onto which music is recorded
mixed	=	combined
loudspeaker	=	a piece of equipment that makes sound louder
groove	=	a cut shaped like a triangle that goes across something
metal	=	a usually shiny substance that carries heat and electricity well; some metals are gold, silver, copper, and aluminum
disc	=	something round and thin
ridge	=	opposite of a groove; the raised part of something
pressing machine	=	a machine that shapes something by squeezing it
plastic	=	a substance that can be bent and shaped many ways but doesn't break easily
melt	=	become liquid when it is hot
flow	=	move
sleeve	=	the inside paper or plastic cover for a record
jacket	=	outside cardboard cover

C. Comprehension

1. What is the difference between the first and the second tape recordings?
2. Why are two metal discs cut to make one record?
3. Why do engineers make a "mother" disc?
4. How is the final record actually made?

D. Analysis

1. What can change music into electricity?
2. Why do you think all the instruments and voices are kept separate on 24 tracks?
3. Why do you think a second tape is made to reduce 24 tracks to 2 tracks?

E. Discussion

1. Sometimes musicians listen to the first recording and then add more instruments or more voices. Why do you think they do this? Couldn't they record everything at once, using more people?
2. The mixer can place some sounds on the left and some on the right, so you hear different things from your two stereo loudspeakers. Do you think this is unnatural? Would you prefer to hear the music as it was played in the studio?

F. Language Practice

1. Describing a Process

A process is usually carried out by people, but it is often described in an impersonal way by using the passive.

The sound **is picked up** by the microphone.
The record **is pressed** by melting plastic.

If you want to use a passive construction with *must* or *have to,* use this form:

must be checked
has to be checked
should be checked

The mother disc must be checked for quality before the record is pressed.

Now describe the process below, using sentences like those above:*

Making Bread

a. wheat/plant/May (must)
b. wheat/harvest/September (should)
c. It/transport/mill
d. It/ground/flour (have to)
e. flour/take/bakery
f. flour/other things/bake/into bread

2. Sequencing

Sequencing words show the order in which things happen. Some were used in Unit 9. Take a minute to look back at them. Here are some other ways to show the order of actions:

Before being mixed together, the sounds are kept separate on 24-track tape.

After being checked, the mother disc is used to make son discs.

Now, using sentences like those above, join together the steps taken in this process:*

  a. the kettle is filled with water / is placed on the burner
  b. the water in the kettle must boil / is taken off
  c. the tea bag is covered with hot water / is put in the cup
  d. the tea bag is taken out and the tea is ready / is left for a minute or two

G. Writing Practice

1. Taking Notes

Before you can describe all the steps in a process, you need to identify all the necessary information. This often means taking notes from a longer text that has a lot of unnecessary information.

Read this text and then make notes, in the form of a list, of the most important steps in the process:

> Papermaking
> Modern paper is made from a mixture of many fibers like rags, linen, wood, and wastepaper. The main ingredient is wood pulp, made from whole trees after the bark has been taken off. The main areas of production are Finland and Canada, where the trees are cut down, taken to the sawmill, and chopped up. The pieces of wood are then ground up and mixed with water to make wood pulp. This is mixed with other substances, such as glue, to make a paper fiber mixture which is then poured out onto wire screens. The screens are large sheets of metal with many holes in them. Here the water is taken out of the mixture, which is then dried and passed through many rollers to press it into shape. This process makes one long sheet of paper, which is wound into a large roll at the end of the manufacturing process.

2. Sequencing

It is important to get the steps of a process in the right order. These steps are out of order. Write them again in the right order and add the correct sequencing words.

Cotton
  a. clothes are made from the finished cotton
  b. the seeds are removed
  c. the cotton is spun into thread
  d. cotton is picked from the bushes
  e. the thread is woven into cloth
  f. it is transported to the mill to be spun

2. Describing Diagrams

Many processes are described by pictures, with the steps written beside the pictures. Using sequencing words, write a describing sentence by each picture to show how to make a cup of tea.

H. Writing Tasks

1. Look at the following pictures that show how tea is produced. Use the pictures and the words below them to write a text describing the tea-making process. Try to combine shorter sentences where possible. Use linking words like:

First,	This is followed by . . .
Second,	In addition,
Then,	The next step is . . .
After that,	The next to the last step is . . .
	Finally,

The introduction and the first sentence of your text are below. Use #10 as the closing for your text.

> Tea comes from the evergreen plant *Camellia Sinensis*. The cuttings are carefully nursed in pots for about 18 months, and then planted in the ground. After five to seven years of careful pruning to the correct height, the young bushes produce a good quality leaf and will continue to do so for half a century or more.
>
> There are ten main steps in the production of tea.

Essential Steps in the Manufacture of Tea

1. Picking or plucking:
   Only two fresh leaves and a bud are picked. These are taken to the factory.

2. Drying or withering:
   The leaves are allowed to dry. It reduces the moisture. The leaves are broken. There are two methods for doing this: Orthodox Rolling, *or* crushing, tearing and curling.

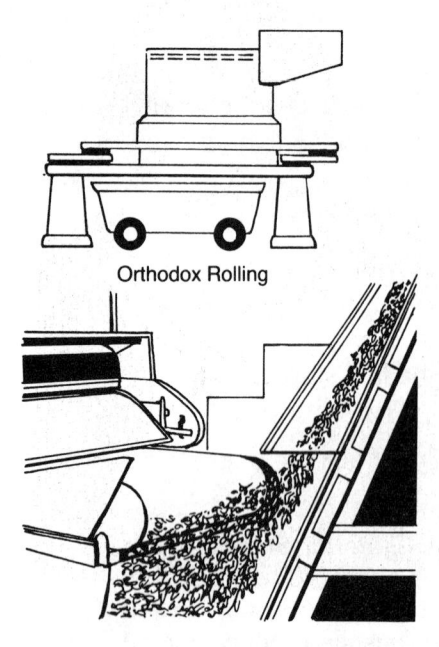

Orthodox Rolling

3. Crushing, tearing and curling:
   This method produces smaller pieces.

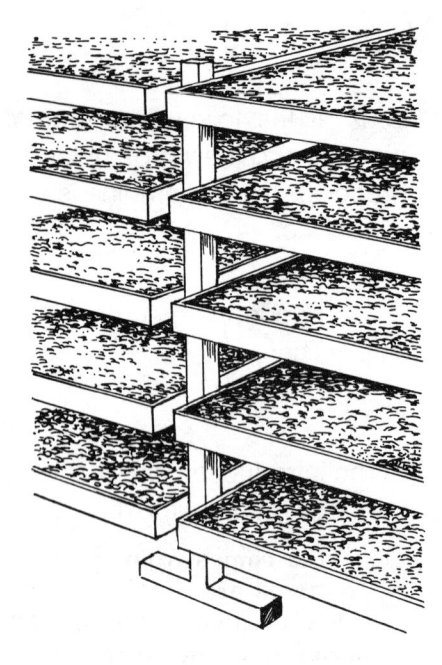

4. Fermentation:
   The leaves are kept in a room under special conditions until they reach a certain color and quality.

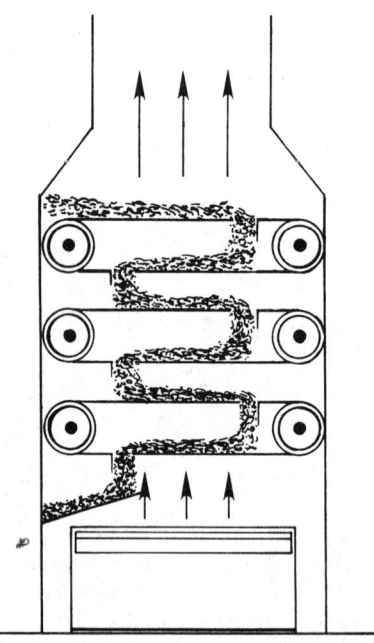

5. Firing or hot air drying:
   The fermentation is stopped by drying the leaves with hot air. This changes their color to black.

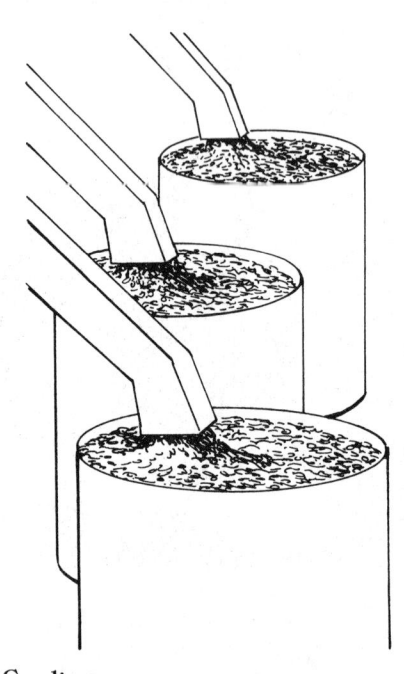

6. Grading:
   The leaves are put into moving sieves. The leaves are separated by size. They are packed into tea crates.

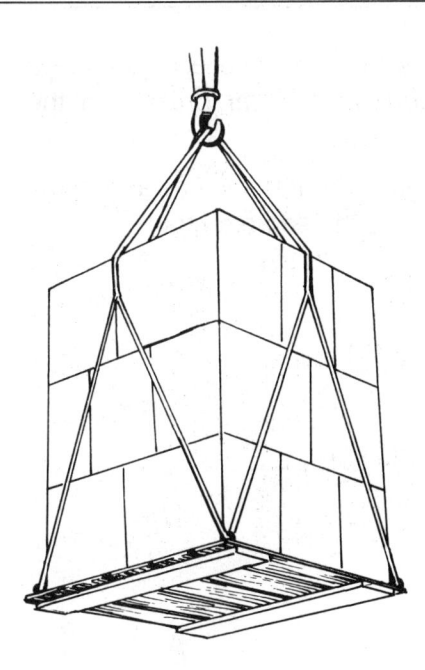

7. Transporting:
   The crates are loaded onto trucks, ships and planes and are shipped to the U.S. and other countries.

8. Tasting:
   Expert tea tasters check the flavor and quality of tea when it arrives in a country.

9. Selling or auctioning:
   Different types of tea are sold at a market. Then they are mixed together, or blended, to make the tea we drink.

10. After reaching the tea-packaging factory, as many as thirty different teas are blended to make such famous brands as Tetley and Lipton. This ensures that tea drinkers' favorite blends are always the same quality.

2. You are going to teach a group of students how to drive a car. Write a description of the process one must go through to start a car, drive it, use the gears and brakes, etc. Keep it impersonal.

3. You are a student in an English language program. Your friend has asked you to write and describe the process for getting into the same course.

17. TELLING A STORY/ NARRATING

A. Text

$1.2 Million Share of Jackpot Was Honest Man's Reward

<u>Canadian Press</u>
MONTREAL

A welfare recipient who was honest enough to return a lottery ticket worth more than $7 million was rewarded when owner Jean-Guy Lavigueur cut him in on the winnings – a share worth $1.2 million.

William Murphy is a 28-year-old welfare recipient who found the Loto 6/49 ticket in a wallet he picked up on a Montreal street Sunday. The ticket, one of several in the wallet, won $7,650,267 in Saturday's draw, the fourth biggest jackpot ever paid in the country-wide lottery.

The wallet belonged to Mr. Lavigueur, a 51-year-old unemployed laborer who was to begin receiving welfare payments this week. Mr. Lavigueur, a widower, his three children, Sylvie, Michel and Yves, and his brother-in-law, Jean-Marie Daudelin, had bought the $1 ticket.

Until Mr. Murphy tracked them down, the Lavigueurs had no idea their lost ticket had won. But Jean-Guy Lavigueur was so struck by Mr. Murphy's honesty that he immediately decided the young man would have an equal share of the winnings along with the five purchasers.

"I put the wallet in a mailbox," Mr. Murphy recalled, still overwhelmed. "But I kept the tickets so I could check them out later. I figured it might be good for $10 or something.

"About four hours later, I was sitting down having a coffee. I'd bought a newspaper and was checking the tickets – and that's when I realized it was worth $7 million.

"I almost had a heart attack," said Mr. Murphy, who is from Vancouver and has lived in Montreal for three years.

Mr. Murphy, who is single and lives in a rooming house in the Montreal suburb of Westmount, had 56 cents in the bank when he found the wallet.

But he soon decided he could not keep the windfall. He remembered the street name and part of the street number of the wallet-owner's address and managed to find the house in east-end Montreal on Sunday evening.

"He came to our house and said, 'You're a millionaire,'" recalled Mr. Lavigueur, who had lost the wallet as he got out of his car on Saturday night. "I told him to come in, but I didn't believe him until I saw the ticket.

"And I said to him, 'I'm giving you $1 million.' How many honest people are there around these days? Well, we've just seen there are still some left."

[Globe & Mail, April 2nd 1986 pA1]

B. Glossary

share	=	a part
jackpot	=	money you can win as a prize
honest person	=	a person who tells the truth
reward	=	money given to someone who returns something that has been lost
welfare	=	money the government gives to poor people
recipient	=	receiver
lottery	=	a competition in which people buy tickets with numbers on them, and the person whose number is picked gets the prize
cut him in on	=	gave him part of
wallet	=	what you keep your money in
draw	=	the time when the winning number is picked
widower	=	a man whose wife has died
tracked them down	=	looked for and found them
struck	=	felt strongly
purchasers	=	buyers
overwhelmed	=	too much feeling; more feeling than one is ready for
heart attack	=	damage to the heart when not enough blood reaches it
rooming house	=	a house where people rent rooms
windfall	=	money you find or win unexpectedly

C. Comprehension

1. Where did Mr. Murphy find the wallet?
2. Whose wallet did Mr. Murphy find?
3. What was Mr. Lavigueur's job?
4. How many people bought the winning ticket?

D. Analysis

1. How many people shared the prize?
2. Why did Mr. Lavigueur give Mr. Murphy $1.2 million?
3. Why did Mr. Murphy keep the tickets when he put the wallet in the mailbox?
4. Why did Mr. Murphy "almost have a heart attack"?
5. What do you think makes the story special?
6. What is the lesson to be learned from this story?

E. Discussion

1. What would you have done if you had found the winning lottery ticket?
2. What would you have done if you had been Mr. Lavigueur?

F. Language Practice

1. Describing Feelings

Here are some of the words we can use to describe how people feel or react to a situation:

Positive	Negative
excited, excitement	shocked
lucky	horrified
thrilled	frightened
happy	terrified
relieved	apprehensive
grateful	worried
glad	nervous
proud	scared
	disappointed
	sad

When telling a story that involves people, we often include a description of how they feel. Use some of the words above to complete a story about a first parachute jump. Try to make the story as interesting as possible by choosing your words carefully.

"I was a little _____ before we went up in the plane, because I knew it was dangerous. The others were a little _____ too, but also very _____. I wasn't _____ when I jumped, and for the first few seconds I felt _____ that I had the courage to try. When I realized the parachute didn't open I was _____, and thought about what it would be like to hit the ground. I was _____ that I would soon be dead. I don't remember much more until I woke up in a hospital. I'm very _____ to the doctors and nurses there – they were nice. I'm very _____ it's all over, and not _____ that I didn't have time to enjoy the jump properly."

2. Intensifying

Some words seem stronger than others, although their meaning is really the same, or nearly the same. When you are telling a story, the words in the right-hand column help to make it more interesting:

Neutral	Strong
to jump	to leap
to break	to smash
to pull	to jerk
to fall	to plunge
to go	to race
quick	instant
fear	horror
unbelievable	incredible

Use some of the strong words to make the text below more interesting:

> Jack Kravitz was driving down one of Maine's highest mountains when he realized that his brakes weren't working. A look of fear came to his face. He tried the emergency brake, but nothing happened. It was unbelievable, but true. He couldn't slow down the car. He had to make a quick decision. He opened the door, jumped out, and rolled onto the road. As he lay there he saw the car go downhill very quickly, and then fall over the edge of a cliff. He couldn't see anything, but he heard it break into a thousand pieces at the bottom of the mountain.

G. Writing Practice

1. Setting the Scene

An important part of telling a story is the beginning. It must get people interested. There are two ways to start a story. One is to describe the scene itself: the place, time, weather, people involved. The other is to give the reader a "taste" of what the story is going to be about. This is done in the text at the beginning of the unit:

> "A welfare recipient who was honest enough to return a lottery ticket worth more than $7 million was rewarded when owner Jean-Guy Lavigueur cut him in on the winnings – a share worth $1.2 million."

Now try the second method. Rewrite the beginning of the following text to give a "taste" of what is going to happen:

It was a beautiful summer day, and hundreds of tourists were enjoying breakfast in the airport's restaurants. Many who watched the planes coming and going saw a jumbo jet speed down the runway and take off. As they turned to watch it climb, there was a scream of horror. Another plane had appeared out of nowhere and was flying across the path of the jumbo jet. Thanks to the quick thinking of the pilots, a major tragedy was avoided.

Now try the first method on the lottery story. Write an introduction that describes the scene.

2. Creating Suspense

Suspense is the feeling of not knowing how a story will end. It creates excitement and interest. You can do this by leaving important information until the end (not like the lottery story, which tells you almost everything at the beginning). So it's not always a good idea to give a "taste" of what is going to happen – that can spoil the suspense.

To practice this, write a short summary of the lottery story giving the basic facts. But don't explain that Mr. Murphy got $1 million, or exactly how things happened, until the last two or three sentences.

3. Personal Accounts

The short texts above are mainly impersonal. It is usually more interesting if a story is told by someone who was there, or who is describing what they themselves have seen or done. Personal accounts use 'I' instead of 'he', are more informal, and describe feelings more strongly. For example, look at this sentence from the text on Jack Kravitz:

A look of fear came to his face.

Jack can't write this about himself, so he would write:

I was terrified.   or   I felt very frightened.

Now practice this by rewriting the story below about Nick and Anna trying to sell their house. You are Nick or Anna. Explain what happened:

Lucky for Some ... It's No. 12A
by Carlos Alverez

Nick and Anna di Pietro hoped to sell their modern house quickly ... until their number came up.

The house on Wilton Avenue in Wilmington, Delaware, seemed a bargain at $149,000 and there were plenty of interested buyers.

But each inquiry dried up when Nick revealed that the number of the house was 13.

Then the number was changed to 12A and Nick and Anna sold it the next day.

H. Writing Tasks

1. Write the story of some event that *you* have experienced – a disaster or a good experience, or something humorous.

2. Imagine you have interviewed someone famous. Now write the story of this person's life.

3. Read this newspaper report, and then rewrite it as a personal account from Sam's point of view. Include conversations he might have had with people.

SMASH HIT HERO

Sam Fawzi was a hero in Chicago yesterday, saving two young girls in a runaway car, but wrecking his own car in the process.

Sam, a mechanic from Urbana, Illinois, was driving past a Pontiac parked outside a supermarket when he saw it start to roll slowly down the hill. Inside the car were two young girls in the back seat – but no driver. Sam stopped quickly, jumped in front of the Pontiac and tried to stop it by pushing against the front of the car. Another passerby jumped into the car and put on the brakes, saving the girls from certain injury.

It was at this point that Sam noticed his own car rolling slowly down the hill – and going too fast for him to stop it. It crashed into a parked bus at the bottom of the hill, and was so badly damaged that it had to be towed away to a garage.

As if this was not bad enough, Sam now finds he has no one to blame. He was so busy chasing his car that he didn't get the name of the driver of the Pontiac, who came out of the supermarket and simply drove away.

18. EXPRESSING OPINIONS

A. Text

WARM OATS: LONG NIGHT

The good releases couldn't go on forever, so here's a really bland one to balance the picture. Warm Oats is one of the greatest bands in the history of rock, but with their last few albums they have clearly run out of inspiration. This one is the worst yet. Their single "There It Goes" is a faster, disco-ish remake of the song "Sleepy Sunday" from their classic and is pretty awful. Heard on the album, it comes over as one of the better tracks. Most of the first side is slow, gentle, slushy and soporific.

It's pleasant, certainly, if you want to fall asleep or need insipid but well-performed background music. But it's not what the wonderful Warm Oats used to be about.

B. Glossary

release	=	a record
bland	=	boring, uninteresting
album	=	record with more than one song on each side
run out of	=	no longer have any
inspiration	=	ideas
disco-ish	=	discotheque-style music
remake	=	a new version
comes over	=	gives the impression, seems to be
tracks	=	songs
slushy	=	sentimental (in a negative way)
soporific	=	puts you to sleep
insipid	=	weak, with no character

C. Comprehension

1. What does the writer think of Warm Oats' new record?
2. What did the writer think of Warm Oats before this record?
3. What is the difference between "There It Goes" and the other songs on the album?
4. What good things does the writer say about the music?

D. Analysis

1. What is the purpose of a text like this? Where do you think it comes from? What is the name for it?
2. What does the writer think is the problem of Warm Oats? Why has the writer's opinion changed?
3. How do you find out the writer's opinions about the group and the music? Underline the parts of the text that express an opinion.
4. What is meant by *a classic*?
5. The writer says, "It's not what the wonderful Warm Oats used to be about." What do you think the writer feels they *used* to be about?
6. What type of rock music does the writer seem to like?

E. Discussion

1. What do you think is the purpose of criticism like this? Is it to help people choose records? Is it to make the critic famous?
2. Is it possible to describe music in words like this? Do you take any notice of criticism or reviews before you buy records?
3. Some people would say it is a waste of time to write a review of a pop record, because pop music is not serious and only lasts a few weeks. What do you think of this viewpoint?

F. Language Practice

1. Expressing an Opinion

If you think something is good, you can express your opinion in a simple way, like this:

It's good.

To make it clear that this is *your* opinion, and to make your conversation and writing more interesting, there are several phrases you can use to introduce your opinion:

I think that . . .
In my opinion, . . .
I would say that . . .
As far as I'm concerned, . . .
The point is that . . .

Now use the above phrases to give your opinion on these topics:

a. people flying to the moon
b. drinking alcohol
c. vegetarianism
d. rock music

2. Tentative Opinions

If you are not sure of your opinion, or if it's not very definite, you can use these words and phrases to show it:

Perhaps it's a question of . . . (formal)
I'm not sure that . . .
Some people would say that . . .
Maybe the reason is . . . (informal)

Now practice using the above phrases. Give a tentative (unsure) opinion on these topics:

a. strikes
b. killing animals for fur coats
c. nuclear power
d. the need for homework at school

G. Writing Practice

1. Analyzing Opinions

As well as expressing your own opinion, you must be able to understand the opinions other people are expressing. Look at the two texts and one cartoon below, and write a description of the opinion that each writer is expressing, or what you think he or she is expressing. In each case, explain what it is that makes you think this is the opinion the writer had.

a. What does the writer think about the movie *A Room with A View*?

> ***½ [unrated] *A Room with a View*. This visually ravishing, sophisticated and literate adaptation of E.M. Forster's novel, set in turn-of-the-century England and Italy, is a romantic comedy of manners that respects the viewer's intelligence. First-rate cast includes Helena Bonham Carter, Julian Sands, Maggie Smith, and Denholm Elliott.
>
> — Janice Finlay
>
> from *Newsday*, Sunday, May 24, 1987 (Pt. 2, pg. 9)

b. Here is a critic's opinion about another album. What does the writer think about this record? How is this opinion different from the opinion in the text at the beginning of the unit?

> The sound of the album is beautiful, because the band has always written with a love for beautiful changes, because the harmonies are as well-sung as ever, and because the production, by Jim Guercio and Bruce Johnston, strives unashamedly to please the ear. The song which has received most attention is "Here Comes the Night," a ten-minute disco version (with added arrangements by Bob Esty) of the tune from "Wild Honey."
>
> The rest of *L.A.* is comprised of short, melancholy, exquisite ballads. "Angel Come Home" is a great pop record on an old theme. "Good Timin'" and "Full Sail" are songs with positive messages that make you feel sad; it's clear how imperfect we are, how pathologically misunderstanding and misunderstood, how seeing the light and employing it are not the same thing. That they communicate irony without bitterness, sadness without hopelessness, is the mark of their art.
>
> Davitt Sigerson

c. What is the cartoonist's opinion about libraries, the people who work there, and people who read books? What does he want you to think?

2. Responding to Opinions

When you read or hear other people's opinions, you usually want to respond by giving your own opinion about the same subject. You can do this by agreeing or disagreeing (see Unit 19) or by simply stating what you think and letting other people analyze whether you agree or disagree. For example:

Opinion: I think all murderers should be hung.
Your opinion: I think the real problem is finding out why people commit murder in the first place.

Here are some useful phrases:

The main point is . . .
The *real* problem seems to be . . .
I tend to think . . .
What we *should* be worrying about is . . .

Practice responding in this way to the following opinions. Write your opinions as if they were a letter to a newspaper or magazine.

a. Government documents should be available for everyone to see.
b. All children should stay at school until they are eighteen.
c. No one should be allowed to have more than one house or one car. The world is too short of resources.

H. Writing Tasks

1. Give your personal opinion about a film or concert you have seen, and advise someone else to see it or not to see it.
2. Choose a favorite book or record and write a serious (formal) review of it, explaining why it is good.
3. You have just been to a football game or similar exciting sports event. Write a letter to a friend who likes the same sport, telling him or her about the game.

19. AGREEING & DISAGREEING

A. Text

B. Glossary

gibble	=	an invented word replacing the name of things to buy, things to learn, things to believe, etc.
rush out	=	hurry out
heed	=	pay attention to
raise	=	bring up
fellow Americans	=	people who are American citizens just like the speaker
cults	=	groups of people who believe the same thing, often a religious group
threat	=	possible problem or danger
mind control	=	getting people to think a certain way by always telling them how to think

C. Comprehension

1. How are the television, the teacher, the priest, etc. alike? What are they doing?
2. What is happening in each picture?
3. What are the people learning in each situation? What does the cartoonist think they are learning?
4. What is happening to the two children in the eight pictures? What is this supposed to show?
5. At one point the young man and woman are shown separately. Why is this?

D. Analysis

1. Look again at each picture and summarize what is happening to the children. Try to think of a word or words that could replace "gibble."
2. What does the cartoonist think has the strongest influence in everybody's life?
3. The text of the last picture has an implied, or hidden meaning. What is it? What is the cartoonist saying?
4. *Irony* can be described as the difference between what is expected in a situation and what actually happens. The title of the TV program, "Cults and the Threat of Mind Control," is ironic when compared with the rest of the cartoon. Explain why.

E. Discussion

1. Do you think TV, teachers, the church, and magazines try to influence how we think? Is the cartoonist's idea a good one, or an exaggerated one?
2. A lot of people watch TV all the time, like the people in the cartoon. Does that mean they agree with everything they see or hear all the time? Do you?

F. Language Practice

1. Agreeing

Agreeing is showing a positive response to someone's opinion, even if it's just nodding your head. But when you're writing, you want to show that you agree with something that was said or written before. So you need to restate the opinion:

I agree that football is a waste of time.
My opinion is the same as Mr. Smith's, who says that all rock music is garbage.
I support the people who want to change the drinking laws.
I'm with Tim, who says that tennis is great to watch on TV. (informal)

Now use the above sentences to agree with and restate these opinions from a radio discussion program:*

a. No family should have more than two children.
b. All education should be free.
c. There should be no borders between countries.
d. "English should be taught in all schools," says Mr. Loftus. (informal)

2. Disagreeing

In both speaking and writing, disagreeing is a more difficult task than agreeing. It is important to decide how strongly you disagree and how to express that disagreement. You must consider the status or positon of the person you're disagreeing with. You can be more direct with a friend than you can with someone who's in a higher position than you or who you don't know very well.

In addition, when you are writing, you need to restate the opinion with which you're disagreeing so the person you're writing to can understand how you feel. Here are some examples (from strong to weak):

You're wrong when you say that . . .
I can't believe you think that . . .
I think you're wrong to believe that . . .
Do you really believe that . . .

Now practice using the above sentences by disagreeing strongly with these opinions. You live in a student residence and have been to a meeting where the following changes were suggested. Write a note to the residence committee disagreeing strongly.

a. to make the residence co-educational (boys and girls living in the same building)
b. to get rid of the curfew (the time when everyone has to be inside the residence)
c. to make the washrooms unisex (boys and girls using the same washroom)

G. Writing Practice

1. For and Against

When you are discussing or writing about a subject, you can often divide the opinions and arguments into two groups: "For" and "Against," the good points and the bad points of the topic.

For example, here are the arguments and opinions we could put under "Against" if we write about the subject of television:

<u>Against</u>
- TV influences how we think.
- TV advertisements tell us what to buy.
- Watching TV means sitting down – it's unhealthy.
- Watching TV stops people from thinking for themselves or making their own entertainment.

a. Now make a list of arguments about the good points of television.

b. Make a table of "For" and "Against" points for two of these topics:

frozen foods
sports cars
jogging

2. Below is a list of comments regarding the killing of whales. Write full sentences showing that you agree or disagree using different expressions.
Killing whales is cruel.
Killing whales is unnecessary for all cultures.
Whales are dying out. There are not many left.
Killing whales disturbs the balance of life in the sea.

H. Writing Tasks

1. Write a letter to your friend agreeing or disagreeing that it's better to own a motorcycle than a car.

2. It's better to have a job with a lot of free time but not much money, than to have a job with a lot of money but not much free time.
Write a formal composition to agree or disagree with this opinion. Explain the advantages of your viewpoint.

3. This letter appeared in the newspaper. You disagree with it very strongly. Write a reply addressed to the editor of the newspaper. It should be a formal letter. Address it to: Editor, Los Angeles Sun-Times, P.O. Box 299, Los Angeles, CA.

Dear Editor:

I think it is disgusting that this town has increased the cost of using the parking lots. It is already very difficult to park anywhere, because of the stupid "No Parking" signs. We pay a lot of money in taxes for streets, then the government stops us from parking on them so that silly pedestrians can go shopping.

We should be allowed to park anywhere for free, and drive anywhere in the city. Cars need more freedom!

Jackie Ewing
Los Angeles

20. BUILDING AN ARGUMENT

A. Text

Single, Solvent, and Fancy-Free

There are many good reasons for being single. One of the best reasons for being single is the freedom it gives you to spend your own money in your own way. Wine, women, and song – in that order – seem to account for a great deal of men's salaries, while women spend their money on clothes, cosmetics, and males.

Another good reason for being single is that single people have very few responsibilities. Singles do not have the chores of family shopping or doing odd jobs around the house. They don't spend their time worrying about babysitters so they can get out one night a week.

Singles are free to spend their time just as the mood strikes them. They can roller-skate, go to the movies, explore old ruins, or just sit with their feet up and enjoy the innocent sin of being completely lazy. They can go to bed when they like and get up when they like. They can eat where, when, and what they want, and meet whomever they like as often as they like.

Single people are very lucky financially. And the freedom is great. If you don't believe it – ask a married friend.

B. Glossary

solvent	=	without money problems
fancy-free	=	with no worries
cosmetics	=	makeup
chores	=	boring household jobs
roller-skate	=	to glide along a sidewalk or floor on footwear with wheels
ruins	=	what is left of very old buildings
innocent	=	harmless

C. Comprehension

1. Who is the writer comparing single people with? Which group does he think has a better life?
2. What are the main reasons for staying single?
3. What can single people do that married people can't do? Is that really true?
4. What does the picture suggest about single life? Is it realistic?
5. What does the writer suggest you should do if you don't believe him? Why?

D. Analysis

1. Do you think the writer is single or married? How can you tell?
2. What group of people is this text written for? What do you think the purpose is? Is it to persuade people to stay single?
3. This text is actually part of an advertisement for a computer dating service. The service will take details about you and find friends of the opposite sex for you – if you pay the charges. Why do you think they start the advertisement by saying how wonderful it is to be single? Wouldn't it be better to suggest you need a husband or wife? What do you think?

E. Discussion

1. The text suggests there is a difference in the way single men and women spend their money. Do you agree? Or is this an exaggerated opinion?
2. Many people pay a lot of money to this computer service in order to find a boyfriend or girlfriend who has the same interests. Why do they do this instead of meeting people normally? What do you think of it?
3. Do you agree that it is better to be single than married?

F. Language Practice

1. Connectors

Some words are very useful to connect ideas together:

Because records have good quality sound, they are better for classical music.

Since records have better sound, they are better for classical music.

Records have good quality sound; **therefore,** they are better for classical music.

Although cassettes are improving, records are still better.

Cassettes are improving. **However,** records are still better.

Each of these words – **because, since, therefore, although,** and **however** – is used in a different way. Look at the examples again and then fill in the blanks in these sentences with the same words:*

Heavy trucks cause a lot of damage to our roads. _____, they are very unpopular. Many people suggest that the goods could go by train _____ trains do not damage roads. _____, not every town has a train station. _____ this sounds like a good idea, it doesn't actually work.

2. These sentences are in the right order, but need to be connected using some of the following words:

> **although   therefore   because   however   but   and**

Make four sentences out of this list by using the connectors:*

many theaters were in danger of closing
most people preferred to stay home

there has been an improvement recently
this improvement has helped many theaters

there used to be good films on TV
people stayed at home

the situation is now very different
the TV bosses will not admit it

G. Writing Practice

1. Planning

When you are writing a composition, you must have a plan. This is especially important if your composition is expressing your opinion, putting forward an argument, or comparing the "For and Against" points of a topic. A good plan makes it easier to write – and makes the composition easier to read. Look at the text again and pick out the reasons for staying single.

Now look at the plan below for a composition titled "Why You Should Stay Single":

Introduction: Many people believe that staying single is better than getting married.
- why it is so popular

Main point 1:   Financial freedom
- what single people do with their money
- compare with expensive married life (babies, houses, etc.)

Main point 2:   Not many responsibilities
- fewer chores

Main point 3: You can do what you want at any time.
- choose what you want to do, and when, where, and with whom you want to do it

Conclusion: If you want to travel, have a good time, and spend money on yourself, it's best to stay single.

2. For and Against

a. From the above plan, you can write a composition. Practice making plans first, by writing a plan like the one above for the following topic:

"Why You Should Get Married"

Some ideas to use are: preventing loneliness, sharing things, fun with children, happy old age.

b. Another sort of plan would be a "For and Against" plan, which brings the two topics together and discusses the advantages and disadvantages, and then comes to a conclusion in the same way. Here is an example:

Title: "Is Marriage Worthwhile?"

Introduction: Many people decide to stay single for different reasons (give examples).

For: Advantages of being single; problems of being married

Against: Problems of being single; good things about marriage

Conclusion: Personal feeling (what I would prefer to do)

Now practice making a plan like this for the following topic:

"Is it worth going to college, or should I get a job after leaving school?"

3. Paragraphing

Using paragraphs instead of one long piece of text makes a composition easier to read. Look at the text at the beginning of the unit.

Each paragraph has a different idea, or a different way of looking at an idea. When you come to the end of a paragraph, there is a natural pause – so it's easier to read.

Practice separating a text into paragraphs by identifying the paragraphs in the text below. It should be five short paragraphs. Put two lines // at the start of each paragraph.*

A battle has been raging at Westbank High School because the principal tried to stop the women teachers from wearing jeans. The battle was won yesterday after the teachers, both men and women, threatened to strike if the women were not allowed to wear jeans to class. The teachers gave three main reasons for their opinion. First, they argued that this was a case of discrimination – that it was very unfair to stop the women from wearing jeans when nothing had been said about the men. They even went so far as to threaten to write to the local newspaper about this. Jeans, they also argued, are not work clothes or the clothes of "slobs," but fashionable casual clothes. Anybody who tried to stop people from wearing jeans, they argued, was years out of date and needed to update their knowledge about fashion. Their final point was that freedom of choice was a basic right of all Americans, and that the principal could not dictate to them what to wear and what not to wear. The principal met with the teachers for more than two hours yesterday and came out of the meeting with a statement that he had been convinced that he was wrong.

H. Writing Tasks

1. Overpopulation and hunger are big problems. Write a plan and a composition about what you think could be done about the problem.
2. "Computers will help us create a much better world in the future." Write a composition agreeing or disagreeing with this idea. Give your reasons.
3. "Should divorce be made easier or more difficult?" Write a composition arguing for the side you believe in.

Answer Key

Unit 1

1. a. Glad you're having a good time.
   b. Hope you can come to the party.
   c. Like some iced tea?
   d. Have any suggestions?
   e. Want a copy?

2. a. I'm saving to buy a car.
   b. She's bought a VCR.
   c. They couldn't help me.
   d. He's very young.
   e. We've found the answer.
   f. They're hungry.

Unit 2

1. a. I like to listen to records but I'd rather go to a concert.
   b. I like to watch TV but I would rather go out.
   c. I like to go to baseball games but I'd rather play baseball.
   d. I like to cook dinner but I'd rather go out.
   e. I like to take a bath but I'd rather take a shower.

2. a. I have been learning Spanish for two years.
   b. Juan has been living in San Francisco for twenty years.
   c. We have been attending this school for ten days.
   d. I have been working in Toronto for a week.
   e. Kim has been playing the guitar for a year.

Unit 3 (Suggested Answers)

a. extremely/very
b. pretty expensive
c. very popular/popular
d. very/pretty
e. pretty intelligent/intelligent
f. very young

Unit 4

a. There are two bathrooms upstairs.
b. There is a guest bathroom on the left in the hallway.
c. There are appliances already in the kitchen.

Unit 5

1. a. The Games were stopped by the Romans in A.D. 393.
   b. Many different games were played by the athletes.
   c. The Games were seen by fifty thousand people in 1896.
   d. The Games were cancelled by the organizers in 1916.

2. a. People used to watch the Games at Mount Olympus.
   b. The Greeks used to stop their wars to go to the Games.
   c. They used to hold the Olympics every five years.

Unit 6 (Suggested Answers)

1. a. The Coral is cheaper than the Bella.
   b. The Bella is not as fast as the Coral.
   c. The Bella comes with power steering, but the Coral has only regular steering.

2. a. The Coral not only has more doors, it has reclining seats as well.
   b. The Bella is not only quieter, it uses less gas as well.

Unit 7 (Suggested Answers)

1. a. Would you like to come on a picnic?
   b. How about going camping for the weekend?
   c. I'm going to the theater on Friday. Would you like to come?

2. a. I'd love to come, but I've arranged something else.
   b. Sorry, but I'm visiting some friends.
   c. That's very kind of you, but I have to work.

Unit 8 (Suggested Answers)

1. a. I'd rather have a Corvette than a Ferrari.
   b. I prefer whole wheat bread.
   c. I'd rather be a politician than an artist.
   d. I'd prefer more money and less time.

2. a. Westerns are interesting, but love stories are very boring.
   b. Beethoven's music is of good quality, but pop music is garbage.
   c. Traveling by car is fast and expensive, but walking is cheap and slow.

Unit 9

Language Practice

1. a. You insert the film into the camera.
   b. You wind the film to number 1.
   c. You set the aperture.
   d. You take off the lens cover.
   e. You look through the viewfinder.

2. a. The film should be inserted into the camera.
   b. The film should be wound to number 1.
   c. The aperture should be set.
   d. The lens cover should be taken off.
   e. The viewfinder should be looked through.

Sequencing

Check the amount of money needed.
Deposit nickels, dimes, or quarters.
Wait until the money drops.
Push the button to make a selection.
If the can does not appear, press the *Coin Return* button.

Unit 10 (*No Answers*)

Unit 11

1. This position offers an excellent salary and provides a good opportunity for the applicant who wishes to obtain experience. We require people who are enthusiastic and hardworking. Sales experience is preferred.

2. a. Having learned Spanish, I want to visit South America.
   b. Having failed his exams, he went back to school.
   c. Having taken the Civil Service test, she went for an interview.
   d. Having taught in a school, he knows a lot about children.

Unit 12

Language Practice
   a. He shouldn't have been following the truck very closely.
   b. He shouldn't have been looking out of the side window.
   c. He shouldn't have been driving without a seat belt.
   d. The windshield wipers should have been working properly.
   e. He should have been concentrating on the road.
   f. The truck should have had good tires.
   g. He should have been driving under 40 mph.
   h. He should have seen the truck stop in time.

Sequencing
   f, b, e, g, a, d, c

Reporting What People Say
   Mr. Smith; 11:19; Mr. Smith said he had heard a loud bang and then had seen the truck skid across the road. He didn't remember anything else after that.

   Mr. Kowalski; 11:19; Mr. Kowalski said he had heard a loud bang and felt the truck start to skid. He thought the wheels had stopped turning. He didn't know what happened after that.

Unit 13

1. a. Henry Fonda, whose acting career lasted many years, received an Oscar for his role in the movie "On Golden Pond."
   b. Boy George, whose hair is now a different color, has just made another hit record.
   c. The Grassy Narrows Indians, whose fish are being poisoned, have complained to the government.
   d. The Blue Jays, whose record last year was very good, are playing good baseball again.
   e. Angie DiBianco, whose friend saved her from drowning, is now recovering in the hospital.

2. a. The workers were warned today about the strike.
   b. New taxes have recently been introduced by the government.
   c. Ten people were killed yesterday in a car crash.
   d. The Prince is engaged to his childhood friend.
   e. The Pope's visit to a synagogue was a great success.

Unit 14 (Suggested Answers)

1. a. If you want to go to college, you ought to work hard.
   b. If he wants to work in the USA, he's got to get a work permit first.
   c. If you want to be successful, you have to get up early.
   d. If they want to make a lot of money, they should start their own business.

2. a. You should go on a diet.
      You should exercise more.
   b. You should be more careful with money.
      Why don't you save a little money each month?
   c. You should check your heating system.
      You could wear warmer clothes.
   d. You should have the battery checked.
      You could buy a new car.

Unit 15 (Suggested Answers)

1. a. Why don't we have a dinner party?
   b. How about camping in Colorado?
   c. Why not try Ladle Soup?
   d. I suggest we meet to discuss business.
   e. Why don't you buy a new TV?

2. a. You'll really enjoy camping. It's terrific.
   b. Don't you think you should go on a diet?
   c. You've got to buy this new record. It's excellent.
   d. You really should learn to play the piano.
   e. Maybe you should buy a new VCR.

Unit 16

1. a. The wheat must be planted in May.
   b. The wheat should be harvested in September.
   c. It is transported to the mill.
   d. It has to be ground into flour.
   e. The flour is taken to the bakery.
   f. The flour and other things are baked into bread.

2. a. Before being placed on the burner, the kettle is filled with water.
   b. Before being taken off, the water in the kettle must boil.
   c. After being put in the cup, the tea bag is covered with hot water.
   d. After being left for a minute or two, the tea bag is taken out and the tea is ready.

Unit 17 (No Answers)

Unit 18 (No Answers)

Unit 19 (Suggested Answers)

a. I agree that no family should have more than two children.
b. I support the people who think all education should be free.
c. My opinion is the same as those who say that there should be no borders between countries.
d. I'm with Mr. Loftus, who says that English should be taught in all schools.

Unit 20 (Suggested Answers)

Language Practice
1. Heavy trucks cause a lot of damage to our roads. **Therefore,** they are very unpopular. Many people suggest that the goods could go by train **because** trains do not damage roads. **However,** not every town has a train station. **Although** this sounds like a good idea, it doesn't actually work.

2. Many theaters were in danger of closing because most people preferred to stay at home.

There has been an improvement recently and this improvement has helped many theaters.

There used to be good films on TV; therefore, people stayed at home.

The situation is now very different, although the TV bosses will not admit it.

Paragraphing

A battle has been raging at Westbank High School because the principal tried to stop the women teachers from wearing jeans. The battle was won yesterday after the teachers, both men and women, threatened to strike if the women were not allowed to wear jeans to class. The teachers gave three main reasons for their opinion. First, they argued that this was a case of discrimination — that it was very unfair to stop the women from wearing jeans when nothing had been said about the men. They even went so far as to threaten to write to the local newspaper about this. Jeans, they also argued, are not work clothes or the clothes of "slobs," but fashionable casual clothes. Anybody who tried to stop people from wearing jeans, they argued, was years out of date and needed to update their knowledge about fashion. Their final point was that freedom of choice was a basic right of all Americans, and that the principal could not dictate to them what to wear and what not to wear. The principal met with the teachers for more than two hours yesterday and came out of the meeting with a statement that he had been convinced that he was wrong.